The Momentum Mindset

How to Overcome Your Inertia and Achieve an Incredible Life!

The Authors

Vicki Main - Director of VLM Training & Coaching Specialists 	Vicki is an entrepreneur, qualified lecturer, Entrepreneurial Mindset Profile® (EMP) Master Trainer, and business coach with over 20 years experience. Fascinated by people, and curious about their dreams, Vicki asks a lot of questions and gets excited when she sees someone reaching their true potential. Born in Gateshead, UK, Vicki is now based between London and Perth, Western Australia, working in both countries to help people create action, grow their businesses and live their best life. www.govlm.com
Jonathan S.Bean  *Photo Credit: Martin Allen Photography*	Jonathan is a successful charity fundraiser, writer, and VLM trainer. He has crafted articles for magazines, written a poem you can sit on (it's painted on a city centre bench in his hometown of Southampton, UK), and raised millions of pounds from charitable foundations for causes ranging from a theatre company to a children's hospice. As a trainer, his area of expertise is helping you to tell your story. www.jonathansbean.com

Dear Bryn,

62/100

Thankyou for your friendship
and for contributing to this
book! I still love your podcast
episode - super inspiring!!

The Momentum Mindset

Best wishes

How to Overcome Your Inertia and Achieve an Incredible Life!

Vicki

Vicki Main & Jonathan S. Bean

Go VLM Publishing

First published in Great Britain by Go VLM Publishing, 2023.
VLM Consulting Ltd, Offa, 106 Cheyne Walk, Chelsea, London, SW10 0DG.

First edition, April 2023 - ISBN (paperback): 978-1-7393678-3-1

Typeset in EB Garamond.
Printed in Great Britain by Mixam, 6 Hercules Way, Watford, WD25 7GS.

Cover design: Design Studio Perth, Western Australia.
Cover images © Shutterstock Illustration.
Globe: Stock Photo ID: 1726215964; Photo Contributor: Denny Boy.
Elephant: Stock Illustration ID: 127926530; Photo Contributor: Lightspring.

Website: www.govlm.com - Contact: enquiries@govlm.com

To all the people who read this book and discover the truth:

You can change your mindset to overcome your inertia, build momentum, reach escape velocity, achieve your goals, and live an incredible life.

Prologue

A woman wakes, shaken by a dream, a nightmare she fears is prophetic. She has known for some time now that something - her environment, her attitude, her actions? - needs to change. But it is scary. Unknown territory. Even though her current situation is a negative one, and she is not living how she wants to live, there is a perverse comfort in maintaining the status quo. It's 'the devil you know.' Change is hard, even if it is a change we desire. This morning is different. Enough is enough.

Plans are drawn up, the target is identified, an inward breath to prime the body and mind. This is the anticipation stage. Rocket fuel ignites, neural impulses fire, the eyes look dead ahead. Flying, striding, gliding. It is difficult. Of course it is. This is the activation stage when the greatest input of energy is required to change the state of being. From stationary inertia to movement.

And then? The old bonds strain and break. Resistance is reduced. A new equilibrium is attained. Sustained momentum. Forward progress. Onward. Higher. Greater. It's not all friction-free, smooth and flawless, as nothing ever is, but the effort to make any necessary course corrections is nothing compared to the initial impulse to begin.

Into space, the target reached, a goal attained. This is the achievement stage. Your life has changed for the better. *It's incredible.*

Foreword

As a young woman, I was full of dreams and aspirations. I imagined a life of excitement, adventure, and success. A life where I'd follow my passions and make a difference in the world. But as the years went by, in my late 30's and early 40's, I felt trapped in a toxic relationship, parts of my life seemed mundane, and I was weighed down by a sense of regret that I'd let my previous dreams slip away. I was frustrated but deep down I knew it wasn't too late to make changes in my life to fulfil my dreams. I was ready to take action, to break free from the shackles that kept me playing small, and to live the life I had always imagined I would. An incredible life full of joy, happiness, success and love.

To the outside world I am a confident, high-achieving woman in business who knows what she wants and isn't afraid to get it. Whilst this is true I felt like I'd fallen behind my peers. Comparison is the thief of joy. I emigrated to Australia eight years ago. I was running two businesses and spent so much time building a career and chasing a dream that it was a great distraction from dealing with my problems. I had forgotten what daily happiness and inner peace was. On reflection, I was often in survival mode. I was so determined to help clients and look after others, I gradually forgot about myself along the way. My work and children were the constants in my life and kept me grounded.

The toxic relationship I found myself in was affecting all areas of my life. I chose to stay in it far longer than I should have. I didn't want to change or leave as it felt way too comfortable and safe, although that was a lie I told myself. I wasn't happy and the situation was far from safe. Sadly, looking back, this impacted my confidence, mental health and my capacity to make good decisions for my children. On reflection, I just wanted a loving relationship and craved companionship. I told very few people what was happening and disguised it from my children to protect them and minimise any upset. In some ways I wish I'd just shared what was going on. I internalised a lot. There was a lot of shame and guilt around this period of my life.

I woke up one morning in a state of panic and thought, 'if I don't make serious changes this is not going to end well'. It was at that moment I reached for my notepad and started to write. I made a list of what I would do if I was the smartest person in the world to change my situation and life for the better. I wrote it from the perspective that others could learn from my experience and wouldn't have to go through what I did. This was to become the framework for this book. It was time to reconnect with myself and finally reclaim my life and get rid of the toxicity. It was time for a fresh start.

It's not all doom and gloom. This book would never have been written if I didn't go through that dark phase. We all have periods in life where it doesn't go as planned, yet sometimes these are the biggest gifts (providing we learn from them). There are many things which I would have done differently, but the past is gone. All I have now are the lessons I've learned and wisdom I can share.

I gave myself permission to put myself first and this led to me creating a new life for myself where I am happy and in a loving, respectful relationship. Reciprocity is our collective mantra. My children are and will always be loved and they are at the heart of major decisions I make. Both of them mean the world to me and always have.

Seven months into my fresh start and this new stage of my life, I met Jonathan Bean at a chance meeting on the Isle of Wight. We shared experiences of how we are living our best lives and this book started to take shape, solidifying from a collection of notes into a completed manuscript.

The Momentum Mindset explains how I became unstuck. I worked on myself, got out of the toxic situations and overcame my inertia. With a momentum mindset, I achieved escape velocity. My co-writer, Jonathan, adds stories, insights, and his experience, too.

Whether you are in business or not, this book is about you living your life to your full potential. Its purpose is to help you establish what your greatest gift and superpower is, how to harness it, and live an incredible life.

If you are going through hell (or just want to change one small aspect of your life) this book is for you.

– Vicki Main, London, February 2023

How to use this book

This book, the one you're holding in your hands, that will help you get yourself unstuck, is yours to do whatever you want with. Feel free to scribble on it, cover it with sticky notes, and fold down the corners as bookmarks. In fact, we'd encourage it.

You can read it in any manner that suits you, but 'deep reading' is a technique you may wish to use. Read the whole book, from start to finish, with a pencil nearby. Whenever you find a passage that resonates with you, or that you would like to return to, mark it with your pencil. Then carry on reading. By marking a section then moving on, you can maintain your reading flow.

When you've reached the end, go back to the beginning and find all your pencil marks. On this second read through, you can take the time to reflect on particular sections, make notes, or jot down ideas. This is also a good time to start the exercises that will take you from being stuck (a state of personal, professional, or creative inertia in which you are unable to reach your goals), through to achieving escape velocity (the point at which the factors that once held you back have been overcome and the momentum of your own success carries you forward toward the incredible life you deserve).

Contents

CHAPTER ONE

You deserve an incredible life

Any action is often better than no action, especially if you have been stuck in an unhappy situation for a long time. If it is a mistake, at least you learn something, in which case it's no longer a mistake. If you remain stuck, you learn nothing.

– Eckhart Tolle, spiritual teacher

Dumbo in Space

In the 1941 Disney animated film, *Dumbo,* the titular elephant learns to fly.[1] Clearly, it's a fantastical proposition, so not to be interpreted as scientifically accurate, but it's a useful metaphor for us to explore.

Jumbo Jr., aka Dumbo, is born with over-sized ears into a family of circus elephants. He is bullied because of the size of his

---

[1] Here's a piece of trivia for any pub quiz fans: the main character's name was actually Jumbo Jr. Dumbo was the nickname given to him.

ears and not given an opportunity to shine. He is dressed as a clown and made to perform dangerous stunts. He has a job he doesn't want, has internalised the negative comments of others, and has low self-esteem as a result. He is stuck in his own state of inertia.

With the support of his friend, Timothy (a mouse), and a group of expert coaches (crows), he explores new possibilities for using his unique talents (his ears) and - against the odds - learns to fly. Making the most of this new skill (his unique superpower) and living according to his values, on his own terms, he is able to live an incredible life.

It's a wonderful, feel-good story, but we wondered, 'what else could Dumbo have achieved?' Imagine that Jumbo Jr. gets a taste for flying and dares to dream of space travel, reaching distant planets. How could he do it? The first step would be to recognise the things that are currently holding him back, and take steps to address them. He may work on his self-belief, identify his motivation for going into space, fill in his knowledge gaps, and gather together a team of experts to help him. They'd build a rocket that was tailored to his needs, wait for a suitable launch window, and ignite the engines. The rocket would rise into the sky, gathering speed. Eventually the rocket would achieve escape velocity, break free of Earth's gravitational pull, and soar onward to new worlds. *Dumbo in space.*

OK, it's a fanciful notion, but beyond the idea of an elephant building a rocket and defying gravity, the process is one that you can adopt to live your version of an incredible life. The rest of this book will explain how.

Come with us if you want to live

We are all born. We all die. These are the only two truly universal events. Between birth and death, we can exist or we can *live*. Beyond that, some of us get to live an incredible life. A life in which we can thrive and soar to great heights. What would such a life look like to you? Whether your dreams are personal, professional, or a combination of both, where do they take you? If you are yet to achieve them, what's stopping you?

In this book, we will take a journey together. We will start by helping you to understand your dreams, and to map out the route to your destination. The end point is up to you; they're your dreams after all. We will give you the insight to identify the external and internal forces that are slowing you down, or getting you stuck in one place. We will provide you with tools and practical exercises to overcome unhelpful thoughts or tricky situations, by adopting a momentum mindset, and achieve the escape velocity required to break free of your negative gravitational pull. With our support, you will empower yourself to create lasting, positive changes.

There are also free downloadable resources available to help you dive deeper and further understand yourself and your purpose. They will also help you develop an action plan for success. These resources have been carefully selected so you can gain a greater insight into who you are, why you do what you do, and what could be blocking your future success. These are available at www.govlm.com/free-resources/

Along the way we will help you establish what your greatest gift and superpower is. Crucially, we will inspire you to give yourself permission to live an incredible life. Because we know - and want you to know, too - that you deserve better.

Steps towards an incredible life

1. Believe you deserve and can have an incredible life.
2. Identify what your incredible life would look like.
3. Recognise your superpowers.
4. Identify what you want to change. What is causing your inertia?
5. Empower yourself to change your mindset.
6. Put steps in place to set the direction and change your situation.
7. Travel light.
8. Build speed.
9. Maintain momentum to achieve escape velocity.
10. Celebrate your hard work and enjoy your incredible life.
11. Repeat the process if you become stuck again.

This is for you

How is it some people achieve their dreams when others do not? If you find yourself pondering this question – perhaps because you're getting stuck and frustrated in the pursuit of *your* dreams – and want an answer you can actually use, this book is for you.

It doesn't matter if you're a business leader or executive, an entrepreneur; yet to get off the start line of work or relationships, on the cusp of a career change or significant life event, or facing challenges in your personal life, we all have things that get in the way or slow us down.

Life will always be punctuated with moments when we feel like we're swimming through treacle, struggling to find the answers we need. We may not be able to find the motivation to take action and change our lives for the better. We might look over and see other people succeeding and suffer sharp feelings of negative comparison that powerfully and adversely affect our self-esteem. We may become so overwhelmed by the challenges we face that we can't see a way to get where we want. This is the opposite to living an incredible life and can affect us all.

Let's return to the question that opened this section: 'How is it some people achieve their dreams when others do not?' It's a big question with a lot of answers. Luck has a big part to play, of course. You can't do anything about the circumstances you were born into, for example. Yet there is a lot you *can* control and plenty you *can* do. With an open mind, you can make your own luck. Vicki's mum always told her, 'You're so lucky. If you fell into the River Tyne you would come out with a salmon in your mouth.' We're yet to test this theory, but this kind of luck isn't something that just happens. It's the result of a positive approach to life that sees the potential in every situation, and dedication towards achieving personal goals.

Every day there are decisions you can make to get another step closer to your dreams. It's a question of having the insight to make the correct decisions, plus the right tools to make the most of opportunities as they arise. This book exists to help you gain that insight and develop those tools, so that you can convert those opportunities into victories.

By recognising and celebrating your successes, your mood and motivation will get a boost. This boost will sustain you through the next challenge. Another victory. Another boost. And so on. The momentum of your own achievements will build and carry you forward. That's the principle at the heart of the Momentum Mindset approach.

In this book, we share real-life experience and practical tips from people who have made changes to their lives and achieved their goals. We will learn how they got out of negative situations to live their best life, on their terms. We'll give you guidance, but you have to do the work. Harper Lee, the writer of *To Kill a Mockingbird*, said, 'Many receive advice, only the wise profit from it.' We've done what we can, by writing and sharing our knowledge, but it is up to you to make the most of it, and put it into action effectively.

Together, we will get you unstuck, moving forward propelled by the momentum of your successes, and living your life to your full potential.

You're not alone

This is not a hustle-culture, bro-science, life-hacking guide. We are not going to show you how to change your life in just a few minutes a day. At the other end of the scale, we're not going to tell you to work 25 hours a day. The answers to any problem are rarely found in the extremes. Big, bold dramatic statements might get people talking about a self-help philosophy, but they rarely offer sustainable advice that works in the real world. This book is different. It's built on the common sense understanding that the key to long-term success is consistent, applied, appropriate effort. Enough effort to make a change, but not so much that you burn out.

Appearing throughout the book are quotes from interviewees featured on the Get Unstuck Fast! Viscosity Podcast, hosted by Vicki. They are professionals working in a variety of fields, who live according to the advice they give. We share their real-life examples and experiences about how they got out of negative situations or circumstances, to live their best life on their own terms.

The Momentum Mindset approach works for people with stressful lives, a lack of time or money, facing difficult professional or personal challenges, or overcoming mental trauma. We know this because every one of the examples we give - plus the thousands of people Vicki has coached - has shown it to be true. This includes the two of us, Vicki and Jonathan.

We both have goals we are yet to achieve, but we have overcome challenges – including those that exist within our own heads – and as much as possible, are living life on our own terms. We're experts at what we do because we've put the hard work in. We're not mystical gurus. We're real people, with real life experience, who may be a few steps further down the road you are about to walk. We're your scouts who have looked ahead to see what lies in your way. We're the guides who will help you find the best route. And we're the cheerleaders who will support you as you dream big and aim high – because, as we said earlier, you deserve it!

Here's a little background. Vicki is a serial entrepreneur, business coach, EMP Master Trainer (more on that later), and qualified lecturer. Fascinated by people, and curious about their dreams, Vicki asks a lot of questions and gets excited when she sees someone reaching their true potential. She has learnt many of the lessons in this book the hard way and wants to share her experience with you.

Born in Gateshead, in the North East of England, Vicki now lives in London, UK, and Perth, Western Australia, working between both countries to help people create action, grow their businesses and live their best life. Her training company, VLM Training and Coaching Specialists, is a consultancy firm that has helped thousands of people to become unstuck, achieve escape velocity, and live an incredible life making the most of their full potential. VLM provides practical training workshops, online programmes, and coaching. The trainers, coaches and mentors who are part of the VLM community have the depth of knowledge and experience to support you and your company's continuous learning and developmental needs, which are essential for your success.

Jonathan is one of the VLM trainers. He loves words. He'd go so far as to say he is addicted to them, unable to walk past a book without picking it up. As a writer and professional charity fundraiser, he has crafted articles for magazines, written a poem you can sit on (it's painted on a city centre bench in his hometown of Southampton, UK), and raised millions of pounds from charitable foundations for causes ranging from a theatre company to a children's hospice. As a trainer, his area of expertise is helping you to tell your story.

As mentioned above, there are useful and inspirational quotes from guests on the Get Unstuck Fast! Viscosity Podcast, featured throughout the book. They are:

- Bryn Walbrook, Freelance Brand Strategist (London, UK).
- Bukamu Dube, Director at Job Skills Training Academy (an experienced vocational education and training professional, leadership and safety specialist) (Perth, Western Australia).
- Paul Edwards, Director at Edwards Commercial Cleaning (Newcastle upon Tyne, UK).
- Caitriona Forde, Founder and Senior Consultant at caIT (specialising in cybersecurity, culture and communication) (Perth, Western Australia).
- Carrie Anne Forsyth, Director at Esteem Dance Company (Perth, Western Australia).
- Dr Christopher Kueh, Design Abilities Specialist (Perth, Western Australia).
- Jo Saunders, Founder, Wildfire Social Marketing (LinkedIn 'demystifier' and marketing specialist) (Perth, Western Australia).
- Karen Dauncey, Managing Director Blue Cherry Online Marketing (Perth Western Australia).
- Karen Dennett, (Founder of Engaging Education) a developer of young entrepreneurs; (Perth, Western

Australia).

- Karen Underhill - Founder of Blue Meanies Arts and Events (Newcastle upon Tyne, UK).[2]
- Tracy Fryer, Director at Design Studio Perth (a branding expert) (Perth, Western Australia).
- Usha Raman, a health and wellness specialist (Perth, Western Australia).
- Will King, Founder, King of Shaves (a guy who bounced back from redundancy by starting a multi-million pound business from his kitchen table) (London, UK).

There are a few other individuals whose wisdom makes it onto the page, including scientists and academics, writers and artists, and a black and white rabbit called Badger.

Life is a series of incremental steps and we all are on this journey of continual learning together.

What are you escaping from?

Much of the time our dreams reveal what it is we *don't* love about our current situation. Dreams of a new job could come from a dislike of your current one. A yearning for romance may be borne from an issue in your current relationship. Fantasising about wide open spaces suggests you are struggling within a stifling, claustrophobic situation.

---

[2] Yes, incredibly, Vicki knows three Karens who are entrepreneurs.

If the meaning of your dreams is not so clear cut, consider their counterpoint. If you want to escape *to* somewhere, where is it you want to escape *from*? The answer will be personal to you. It could range from a relatively minor inconvenience, a life wrinkle that keeps tripping you up, all the way up to an abusive situation you need to quite literally escape from. No matter the severity of your circumstances, before you start your journey towards the life you want and deserve, you first need to assess the one you have.

In the later chapters we will look at ways you can explore this in more detail, but right now the chances are you already know the broad headlines of what it is you want to change. Write it down. Ultimately, you deserve a life you don't want (or need) to escape from, but until we get there, we have to know what we're dealing with. Depending on what it is, seeing it written down may be uncomfortable, but you need to confront it before you can change it. Don't shy away. Look your demons up and down, stare them in the face, and understand what they are and what they look like. Then, you can start to take this situation you want to escape from, and turn it into your launchpad.

> Whatever situation you're in, you need to find a way to step out of where you are and give yourself some time to look at it from a different perspective. Then you can reframe what's happening. Rather than focus on what you want to get away from, you can focus on where you want to go. Ask yourself, 'What would this situation look like in a year's time, if everything was

better? What do I need to do to get there?'
– Karen Dennett, Founder of Engaging Education
(Perth, Western Australia)

Build a life and career you don't want to escape from

We want you to reach a point where you can stop and say, 'I can stop running now.'

Let's clear up what we mean by that. It's not 'I no longer need anything else' as we're not talking about the acquisition and accumulation of skills, wealth, memories or other stuff. The scale of your ambition is for you to decide whether you want a little or a lot. And we're not saying we think you can reach a state of perfection, as that's not possible.

We want you to say, 'I am happy. I am content. My life is incredible.' Aim for this and keep going until you get there. Once you've achieved it, hold on to the feeling and keep it rolling. Maintain the momentum. You can do it.

Why bother?

What would an incredible life look like for you? Close your eyes and picture it. If you're already living it, congratulations! You've nailed it and can put this book down now. But if you're part of the 99.9% (probably) of the population who aren't yet living their best life, be honest and ask yourself: what is stopping you from achieving this right now? We can all come up with explanations as to why we're not living our best lives. 'I'm too busy to develop my side project. Change is scary. I'm not qualified enough. It's not going to work, so why bother?'

But are these valid *reasons* or are they *excuses*? If it's the former, that's OK. Reasons can be overcome. If you don't have the correct qualification, you can go out and train. If you struggle with anxiety, there are things you can do to help reduce or manage that. Excuses are a little trickier because they're not always so rational. They can look like reasons, and they're very closely related, but may have been invented by our subconscious to stop us doing things. Fortunately, excuses can be unpicked to reveal the reason hidden inside them. A fear of failure (a reason), for example, could be hidden behind a statement such as 'It's just not something I've ever felt the urge to try' (an excuse). Once the hidden reason has been identified, work can take place to resolve it.

Change can indeed be scary, and it is often our beliefs and fears that hold us back from making the changes we desire. Our beliefs are the lenses through which we view the world, and they shape our attitudes, values, and actions. If our beliefs are limiting or negative, they can create a self-fulfilling prophecy that prevents us from taking risks or stepping outside of our comfort zones. For example, if we believe that the wildly audacious goal we desire is unattainable, we may shy away from opportunities that challenge us, or we may give up before we even start.

Similarly, fears can also hold us back from change. Fear of

the unknown, fear of failure, fear of rejection, or fear of losing control are all common fears that can prevent us from taking the steps necessary for change. These fears often arise from past experiences, societal pressures, or self-doubt, and they can create mental barriers that make it challenging to move forward.

To overcome these beliefs and fears, it is important to identify and challenge them. This can involve examining the evidence that supports our beliefs and questioning their validity, or reframing our perspective on failure and rejection as recognising setbacks as opportunities for growth and learning. Additionally, building self-awareness, self-compassion, and resilience can help us manage our fears and overcome obstacles on the path to change.

Feel good

We've said it a couple of times already and we'll repeat it again, 'You deserve an incredible life'. Why do you deserve it? Why not? This isn't a transaction. You don't have to earn it. A good life is something you should be able to enjoy *just because*, with no qualifications attached.

The writer, Haruki Murakami, summarised it well, by saying, 'I mean, a life spent doing something you don't find enjoyable can't be much fun, right? [...] What's wrong about feeling good?'[3]

---

[3] Haruki Murakami, *Novelist as a Vocation*, Harvill Secker, 2022.

It's hard to argue with that. There's nothing wrong about feeling good, and this is why you deserve an incredible life. Because we all do! There, we said it again. You deserve an incredible life. We want you to repeat it, too. Even if you don't yet believe it, keep saying it and you'll gradually come to realise it is true. This is the new story for you to tell yourself.

Story-telling

The human mind is a wonderful thing which is capable of amazing feats, but our minds can work against us, too. The inner voice that drives us forwards can also hold us back. We may choose to believe the convenient lies we tell ourselves because it appears easier to do nothing than to do the thing we want. Are you really comfortable with mediocrity, or do you want to act and create change?

Vicki has spent her whole life studying people and has been teaching and coaching for twenty years. In that time she has noticed patterns whereby people often get stuck in self-imposed mental prisons, blocking their chances of success. People remain stuck where they are because they believe stories about themselves and about who they are. Stories that others tell them, but also the stories they tell themselves. Even stories so old you barely remember them, can still echo from childhood through to adulthood. As the writer, Peggy O'Mara, said, 'The way we talk to our children becomes their inner voice.'

Repeated often enough, these stories have the potential to

be so powerful they convince us that it would be more comfortable to remain in a painful situation. Considering an alternative becomes so hard to do that it is easy to feel too overwhelmed to change. Left unchecked, these stories can stop us from taking action and achieving our life purpose.

It takes real courage and bravery to live your best life. You have to be motivated enough, and want it enough to make the necessary changes to achieve it. There will be a grieving process as you leave behind what you once had, even if you never wanted it. You may find yourself wanting your old life back because it is all you've known. Changing your life is tough, so you've got to ask yourself why would you bother in the first place? If you're struggling to answer that question yourself, use our suggestion: 'Because an incredible life is the greatest gift you can give yourself.'

On the other side of fear can be found the most beautiful things in the world. When you find them, all the hard work will be worth it.

> If you've got an idea, go for it. You only live once and most of the time you've got more capability and skills than you give yourself credit for. Don't be afraid. Don't worry about other people. Don't worry about what's going to happen. You'll never know until you try.
>
> – Bukamu Dube, Director at Job Skills Training Academy (Perth, Western Australia)

Put yourself and your happiness at the centre of your universe

It might seem self-centred or even selfish to some, all this self-reflection and talk of living *your* best life. Be assured, it's not. It's about giving yourself power through priorities. You're putting yourself at the centre of your universe and of your happiness, and empowering yourself. It's about assuming responsibility for your own life and not being beholden to others. We're not suggesting you abandon all your obligations or dump those who rely on you. We're aiming to show you that if you always put yourself last, you'll never be first. And if you're never first, you'll never reach your goals. Besides, if you don't reach your goals, your ability to help others will be impaired. It's the same principle behind the emergency safety advice on planes: put your own oxygen mask on first, because if you're incapacitated, you can't help anyone.

This isn't just some manipulated logic or convenient wordplay to justify poor, truly selfish behaviour that negatively impacts others. We do not subscribe to the 'every man for himself' approach to life. Despite what people may say, it is not a 'dog eat dog world.' Where has that expression come from? Dogs don't eat dogs! It's a completely bizarre, false statement, and certainly not a useful life philosophy to live by.

A recurring theme throughout this book is the importance of community and belonging. We have a moral duty to look out for each other and lift everyone up to the same heights we aspire to. When you're happy and flying high, you'll be so much better placed to serve others – whether that support is financial, practical or emotional.

In the next few chapters we will look at self-reflection and how this will support your journey. In order to know where you're going, you need to know who you are first. This book was written to inspire you to increase your self-belief and help you achieve the momentum to overcome the inertia holding you back, so you can achieve your goals. Once you achieve escape velocity, you are forever free. When was the last time you put yourself first? Do it now.

> It's taken me a long time to realise that by not looking after myself, I'm actually doing a disservice to the people in my life, because they're not getting the best version of me. They're getting the tired version, or the overworked version, or the stressed-out anxious version. They deserve to have the happy, vibrant version with the energy to be there for them.
> – Karen Dennett, Founder of Engaging Education
> (Perth, Western Australia)

How to overcome your inertia and get unstuck

How do you get unstuck? Consider this improbable, but illustrative scenario: you've glued your foot to a concrete block and now you can't move. You're not going to get anywhere fast, or build any kind of momentum, with such a hefty weight holding yourself back.

The cause of your inertia is clear (the massive concrete block stuck to your foot!). To rid yourself of the block and get moving again, you have three options:

1. Cut yourself free.
2. Pull hard.
3. Dissolve the glue.

The first option can work. Hack away at the concrete until you can move freely. The risk is some uncomfortable lumps of concrete remain stuck to your foot. You may not notice them at first, but they could cause problems eventually.

Option two is the brute force approach. Don't overthink things, just apply a lot of effort and get it done. It could work, but there's a high probability that you'll leave some skin behind.

Our preferred option is the final one. Take a moment to understand what it is that's sticking you to the block, and find a solution that will dissolve the glue. It will leave both the block and you intact, but separate and able to go your own ways. It's non-destructive and doesn't result in any new problems. All you need to do is identify the glue, and then the solution to dissolve it. Once that's achieved, you can get moving again and build momentum.

In life, some jobs, relationships or personal circumstances are stickier than others. It may take a long time to work out how to dissolve the glue. This book will help you do that.

Activation energy

Here's a science lesson, to help you understand the amount of energy you need to change your life.

A pan of cold water is on the stove. Do nothing and nothing changes. Apply heat, by turning the stove up to max, and something starts to happen. At first, you'll barely notice it. Then a few pin prick sized bubbles will start to form on the bottom of the pan. As the water gets hotter, the molecules move more. The water becomes more agitated and those bubbles are released, climbing to the surface. More bubbles form, now larger than before, and before long the once still water becomes a writhing, boiling mass.

At this point, you can turn the heat down slightly and the water will continue to boil and simmer away, at the same intensity, but with less heat being applied.

This is activation energy at play. To simplify the chemistry involved, activation energy refers to the minimum amount of energy required to get from one state to another. For the pan of water it's the application of heat to get from room temperature up to boiling point. Once the new state has been achieved (i.e. boiling), less energy is required to maintain that new state.

To use another example, imagine you've got to push a car that has broken down. Getting the car moving is hard and you're going to have to put a lot of effort in. Gradually, it will start rolling and the momentum of the car itself will reduce the amount of energy you need to keep it moving.

The same principles apply to making life changes. If you don't put any energy in, nothing will change. Perhaps you'll get lucky or someone else will do the work for you, but the chances of that happening are so minuscule that it's not a viable, winning strategy for success.

Where's the potential for personal growth in sitting back and waiting for a miracle? What lessons would you learn and what experience would you gain? None, or very little. To take the power back and be the CEO of your own life, you need to provide the activation energy. That initial burst of activity has to come from you. This might be difficult, but the pay-off will be tremendous.

It will always take more energy to get from A to B than it will to remain at B. That can be an intimidating prospect. If you're already putting in a lot of energy and focus, yet feel like you're still a long way from reaching your goals (or even going backwards!), the prospect of putting in even more energy is daunting. To cope with this, please remind yourself: This is the activation stage. This is the hardest bit, but once you've reached boiling point, or got the car rolling, you'll be able to ease back slightly and enjoy the results of all your hard work.

It takes a lot of fuel to get your rocket off the launch pad. The boosters will need to keep burning as you work to break free of gravity. Get high enough and the only time you'll have to fire your rockets is to make adjustments to your course or to reach any new destinations you choose for yourself.

Inertia, momentum, and escape velocity

Here's the second science lesson, to explain more of the terminology we use, which is taken from kinematics: the study of motion and the factors which cause an object to move.[4]

Inertia is the notion that an object will not change its location or speed unless the forces acting upon it change. In the context of this book, we are using inertia to describe how a stationary object will not move unless action is taken to move it.

Momentum is the combination of an object's mass and velocity. In practical terms, it explains why a heavy, fast-moving object is harder to stop than a light-weight, slow-moving object.

Displacement is the change in position of an object or person, i.e. the gap between points A and B.

Velocity is the rate at which your displacement is changing, i.e. how fast you get from A to B. Different factors that have an effect on velocity are the amount of power applied, friction and gravity.

When you throw an object in the air it will come back to earth due to the gravitational pull acting on it. Gravity is undoubtedly a good thing. It makes life on Earth possible by keeping us and the atmosphere where we need to be. Quite literally, we would not be where we are without it. Yet there are times we need to overcome gravity, such as leaving Earth to get to space.

To break free of gravity and reach space, an object needs to

---

[4] For the sake of clarity, there is a certain amount of simplification and artistic licence at play here, so it's perhaps best not to copy this section directly into a physics exam paper.

travel at a great enough speed that its upward energy exceeds the downward gravitational forces acting upon it. This speed is known as escape velocity.

In this book, escape velocity is the metaphor by which you will escape the gravitational pull of everyday life and live an incredible life you are proud of. Just like a rocket, you're going to need enough fuel to power yourself to escape velocity. You also need to be travelling at the right time, in the right vehicle, with the right people along the way.

CHAPTER TWO

What do you want?

If you don't like the road you're walking, start paving another one.

– Dolly Parton, musician, singer, philanthropist, absolute legend

What does success look like?

Success and happiness doesn't always look like a nice house, a fast car, and rock-hard abs. More likely, it's something that's harder to see: an internal sense of fulfilment. So often, it is the external indicators of success we are drawn to, but as we'll see below, it is the achievement of intrinsic goals, not external ones, that leads to greater well-being.

The challenge is, we spend too much time comparing ourselves to others without really knowing what our unique gifts are, what we truly want (rather than what we think we want), or even why we exist. As the saying goes, 'comparison is the thief of joy.' It could also be said that 'comparison is a barrier to meaningful self-analysis,' but that doesn't roll off the tongue so nicely. To get to the heart of the matter, and find your intrinsic truth, you're going to have to block out other people's expectations and dig deep into your own idea of success. There are exercises later in the book to help you do this, including the 'So What?' game.

As a foundation, aim to cover these three points when defining what an incredible life would look like for you: autonomy, mastery, and belonging. These are the principles behind Self-determination theory, developed by Edward Deci and Richard Ryan,[5] which explains what humans need in order to thrive. Breaking them down further:

- Autonomy is having a sense of freedom and control over what you do.
- Mastery is the feeling that you are good at something.
- Belonging is being part of a community or something bigger than oneself.

Tick these three boxes, and you'll set yourself up to flourish. Armed with this knowledge, what does your dream look like? Here are three suggestions to show how the SDT concept could be applied:

- Being a freelance (autonomy) writer who is recognised as

---

[5] Edward Deci & Richard Ryan, 'Self-determination theory: A macrotheory of human motivation, development, and health', *Canadian Psychology / Psychologie canadienne*, Vol. 49, Issue. 3, 2008.

an expert in their field (mastery) and engages with a community of readers (belonging).

- Having the time (autonomy) to learn how to cook (mastery) amazing meals your family (belonging) loves to eat.
- Working for a boss who trusts you (autonomy) enough to get on and do great work (mastery) that the whole team (belonging) benefits from.

Your own SDT answer will be personal to you and there are as many possibilities as there are people. Remember, you need all three principles: autonomy, mastery, and belonging. If you focus on just one or two, you run the risk of not quite reaching full happiness no matter how hard you try.

As mentioned above, another key for happiness and improved well-being is to make sure your goals are intrinsic, not extrinsic. Choose goals that relate to how you feel about yourself, rather than how other people feel about you. In practice, that means selecting goals related to personal growth, relationships and health, rather than fame, money or status. Research demonstrates that intrinsic goals improve well-being, whereas extrinsic goals have a detrimental effect.

This is understandable. Extrinsic goals come from ego, insecurity, comparison, and societal expectations. You might get a short term buzz from achieving them, as they'll still trigger all the nice feel-good hormones, but it's not sustainable or long-lasting because it is reliant on external factors. At some point, the buzz will wear off and you'll be left wanting more fame, money or status. It's a cycle that leads to endless dissatisfaction. Intrinsic goals, however, are driven by our internal, fundamental, core values. They're not reliant on anyone or anything other than yourself and your actions. They come from the heart and the soul. Achieve them and you'll get an inner glow that can carry you through the next challenge and beyond.

Realism

We want you to be confident. We want you to dream big, aim high, and believe you can do whatever it is you want to do. Because if you can't do that, achieving the incredible life of your dreams will be impossible.

This confidence needs to be grounded in realism, though. That might seem like we've just pumped up your balloon full of confidence only to pop it before you get started, but that's not our intention.

Instead, we want you to feel confident, but have your eyes open to the possibility that things might not go to plan. You, your intentions, and your actions, are just one part of the equation. There's a lot of other moving parts you don't have any control over. It is helpful to recognise the reality your dreams inhabit, and be open to the possibility that what you want to happen, might not happen. Or, it might not happen in the manner you want it to.

This is true of the big goals, and the smaller daily events that occur along the way. As long as you are moving forward in generally the right direction, and doing so in accordance with your values, you'll get to where you want to go.

> I like the ups and downs of business and the realness of it. I know myself and know that I'm not going to get up every morning and SLAM, start working hard. Sometimes I do, as I'm excited, and that's great, but there are times when the going gets tough and I just have to get through it. Then, it's important to be realistic and break things down to the essentials: What is it I need to achieve today?
> – Karen Dauncey, Managing Director of Blue Cherry Online Marketing (Perth, Western Australia)

> You should not get into business thinking that it's always going to be smooth flowing. There are a lot of times, being in business, when you're dealing with unexpected challenges. You just have to be OK with that and get help if you need it.
> – Bukamu Dube, Director at Job Skills Training Academy (Perth, Western Australia)

Identify your superpowers and you will shine

When was the last time you sat down and identified what your strengths are? When was the last time you sat down and wrote a list of what your unique superpowers are which make you stand out? The things you can do as well as, or better than, anyone else? You are more than capable of shining. You might already be doing so and loving it. You might be doing so and not realising it. Or you might not be shining yet because something is dulling your sparkle. Wherever you're at, please know that you deserve to shine. Identify your superpowers (use the exercise in the next section if you struggle with this), embrace them, and show the world what you are made of.

Golden trophies

What are you proud of? According to some, pride is a sin, so answering this question might not come naturally to you. We would like you to attempt it, though.

If it helps, imagine a trophy cabinet that contains all your achievements. Each achievement has a golden trophy. As you walk along, looking in the cabinet, what are the trophies for? For some, they may be for easily measurable achievements, such as winning a race, being the top salesperson, or passing your driving test. For others, they may be no less important, but tougher to quantify, such as raising children, helping a friend, or overcoming a health problem. The aim of this exercise is not to rank those achievements, or even to try and assign a value to them, but to acknowledge them. This isn't about working out which achievements are more important than others, but recognising that there are good things you have done.

The next level is to look deeper into the true significance

of those achievements and identify the traits and behaviours that led to those successes. For example, did you pass your driving test because you were diligent and made the time to practise regularly? Were you able to help your friend because you were compassionate? Have you displayed patience, persistence, courage, empathy, focus, integrity, or any other positive traits when earning those trophies?

It is these traits we would like you to recognise and celebrate, because these are within you. They can be repeated, scaled up, or applied to any situation, regardless of the context. These are the gold nuggets that made your trophies. They're the greatest gifts you can share with others. They're your superpowers. Harness them, and you can achieve escape velocity.

> Anything that says 'Keep it up, keep going' is always great. But you want to look at the areas where you can grow, too.
>
> – Bryn Walbrook, Freelance Brand Strategist
> (London, UK)

Time for happiness

In a recent conversation, a friend reminded Vicki that happiness is an inside job. That is, it requires you to put some work in, as you can't always rely on others to make you happy. Reflecting on this thought, Vicki wrote a list of all the activities she loves to do outside of work. Some of the highlights include taking part in a comedy course, yoga classes, sailing with friends, and spending time with family and her puppy, Leo. As much as she enjoys building her business, it's vital to connect with others to create happiness and joy in other ways too. (The added bonus is that time well-spent outside of work can benefit your work, too. Some of Vicki's best business ideas have evolved from a spark of inspiration first felt on a yoga mat.)

When was the last time you did something for yourself that you love? Or put yourself first? If this is an area you've neglected, consider this a gentle reminder to go and start that course you've always wanted to do, or get out and meet new people doing something you love. Make yourself happy.

If there is *nothing* at all that gets you excited, gives you a sense of achievement, or makes you happy, perhaps you're not doing *anything* difficult enough. The philosopher, Alan Badiou, wrote:

> Happiness is the subjectivity of a difficult task: coping with the consequences of an event and discovering, beneath the dull and dreary existence of our world, the luminous possibilities offered by the affirmative real, of which the law of this world was the hidden negation. Happiness is enjoying the powerful and creative existence of something that, from the world's point of view, was impossible.[6]

Badiou has a poetic turn of phrase, though it can make it tricky to work out what he is saying. We don't completely agree with

---

[6] Alan Badiou, *Happiness*, Bloomsbury, 2019.

Badiou's viewpoint - as we think there is a lot of happiness to be gained from simple pleasures that don't require any struggle - but there is a truth to what he says. The accomplishment of a difficult task *does* make you happy. The harder the task, the greater the reward. This is why people find enjoyment in physical challenges or learning a new skill. Because they take the impossible (or even just slightly tricky) and turn it into a success.

For a long time, Vicki wanted to do stand up comedy and push the boundaries of what she felt comfortable with. She wanted to demonstrate to herself that she could do it. So she attended a course and (at the time of writing) has completed two stand up performances now at The Comedy Store in London under the guidance of professional comedian Mike Gunn. She absolutely loved the experience. Yes, it was scary, but it was about the journey and proving to herself that she could do it.

It's not just about the summit

We've written about setting goals and having an idea of what you want to achieve, but we have to make something clear: your goals shouldn't just be the endpoints. They should also be the waypoints.

That is, you have to ensure there are things to enjoy and goals to achieve along the way. It's a cliché (but true) to say, 'It's about the journey, not the destination.'

The destination might be just one fleeting moment. If it takes you years to get there, it's going to be a long, hard slog if there are no intermediate goals to enjoy along the way, or if you don't enjoy the work itself. If those intermediate goals can be reframed and redistributed as a constant stream of positive moments, then your whole life becomes enjoyable. Another true cliché: if you love your job, you'll never work a day in your life. If the act of achieving your goals is enjoyable, then not only are you more likely to stick it out and achieve your goals, but you'll enjoy yourself along the way.

We like the following quote:

> To live only for some future goal is shallow. It's the sides of the mountains which sustain life, not the top. Here's where things grow. [...] But of course, without the top you can't have any sides. It's the top that defines the sides.
>
> – Robert Pirsig, author[7]

The quote is from the philosophical classic, *Zen and the Art of Motorcycle Maintenance*, and we think it perfectly summarises the relationship between the journey and the destination.

The conflict between attachment and authenticity

Attachment is the desire to receive approval and recognition from others. Authenticity is the desire to live according to your

---

[7] Robert M. Pirsig, *Zen and the Art of Motorcycle Maintenance*, Harper Collins, 1974.

own principles and beliefs. Ideally, these two things would be in alignment. The things you do, and the people in your life, would all be compatible with the fundamental values deep within your heart.

The well-known psychiatrist, Dr Gabor Maté, explains that unhappiness or inner turmoil can arise when these factors aren't in alignment and we choose attachment over authenticity. That is, problems occur when we prioritise the approval of others over our own self-approval.

There will always be certain scenarios in which the desire for human connection is more important than living according to our values. For example, in a survival situation you may have to attach yourself to people you don't agree with in order to stay alive. But where you have a choice, it is almost always better to opt for authenticity over attachment. Authenticity leads to happiness, and the world needs more happy people.

It relates to business, too. Just finding something to sell, that you don't care about, is not likely to be a path to happiness, as it is inauthentic. Instead, find something you truly care about and do that. Be true to yourself, rather than bend to fit others. Trust that if you put your heart into something, others will see that and want to get involved.

CHAPTER THREE

Who are you?

Your beliefs become your thoughts,
Your thoughts become your words,
Your words become your actions,
Your actions become your habits,
Your habits become your values,
Your values become your destiny.
                    – Mahatma Gandhi, lawyer and ethicist

How do you describe yourself?

We've mentioned intrinsic motivators, but not everyone knows what theirs are, though. That's because they don't know *who* they are, let alone what motivates them. Almost everyone can come up with a list of adjectives to describe themselves, using words such as: introvert, parent, old, funny. They may add in a job title: electrician, teacher, lawyer, pilot. It's also possible they refer to themselves according to their preferred leisure activities:

runner, dancer, artist, gardener. These can all be helpful, but it pays to be wary of relying too much on such descriptors, as they can come loaded with unhelpful, limiting preconceptions.

The first category tends to be 'relative descriptors'. That is, they can be seen as a means of comparing yourself to others: Introverted compared to more extroverted people; someone else's parent; older than people who are younger; or funnier than other people. This can be OK if the relative descriptors are ones we take to be positive. It can be reassuring or uplifting to think of ourselves as clever, entertaining, or energetic, for example. But the reverse is true, too. If the relative descriptors are negative, they can get us down. Very few people like to think of themselves as stupid, boring, or tired, for example. With a global population of 8bn people (and growing!), there will always be someone, somewhere on this planet, whose comparative attributes will be better than yours. Comparing yourself to others can make you feel good, but unless your self-confidence is cast-iron rock solid, it can lead to self-doubt and negative thoughts. You don't have to leave all comparative descriptors behind, as some are helpful and positive, but be aware of the potential problems.

The second category of 'professional descriptors' carry fewer risks, as they tend not to be loaded with emotion, but they can carry implied values which may get in the way of us becoming unstuck and working towards our goals. For example, if you currently work as an accountant, and your identity is tied up with ideas of what being an accountant entails, you may struggle to think of yourself in any other terms. If you're an accountant who wants to be a graphic designer, for example, the struggle to break free of your identity as an accountant could make it tricky for you to think of yourself as a graphic designer and take the plunge to switch careers. Even worse is when we allow other people's negative value judgments to influence the story we tell ourselves. These often include the word 'just'; in these instances taken to mean 'only', or 'limited to'. 'I can't be an entrepreneur, because I'm only a nurse.' Or 'I'm just a teacher, I could never be a chef.' This kind of thinking is often hard to shift because it is so deeply ingrained in our culture. It finds its way into the language we use, which influences how we think. To counteract and break the spell of these stories, to re-programme your thinking, you're going to have to be very careful of the language you use. Never use the word 'just' in this way when describing yourself or others.

The third category, of 'identity descriptors' (i.e. related to our hobbies and interests) are reasonably benign. There's no reason why being a stamp collector should get in the way of being a doctor. Being a vegetarian and opening your own nail bar are not mutually exclusive. There is still a risk to be aware of though. What happens if you identify yourself as being a badminton player, but break your wrist and can't play anymore? Ideally, your self-image will be strong enough that it can withstand this disappointment without losing sight of the value of everything else in your life. This can be difficult, especially if our social lives are tied up in an activity. There can be a fear that 'Without badminton, I don't know who I am'. It's OK to grieve the loss of something you love doing, but please remember that you, and your potential, are so much more than whatever it is you currently tend to do with your time.

I never saw myself as an entrepreneur, and had never even used that word, before Vicki became my mentor. It gave me so much more confidence to embrace that entrepreneurial mindset and not just say 'I'm a dance teacher'. I now know I'm so much more than that.

– Carrie Anne Forsyth, Director at Esteem Dance Company (Perth, Western Australia)

You are unique

Comparison is natural. There may be lots of people you are similar to, or a little alike, at first glance. Look closer and you'll realise everyone is unique, like a snowflake or fingerprint. This includes you.

You have your own personality, experiences, skills, relationships, likes and dislikes. Recognising this is liberating. If you are unique it stands to reason that your path through life can be unique. If someone else's plan isn't working for you, perhaps it isn't the right one for you.

As the world expert in being you, you are the best placed person to define that path. By all means, take inspiration from others as there are a lot of positive examples you can learn from, but don't be afraid of deviating when it is right for you to do so. As the jazz legend, Thelonious Monk said:

I say, play your own way. Don't play what the public wants. You play what you want and let the public pick up on what you're doing; even if it does take them fifteen, twenty years.[8]

Stay true to yourself.

Identify your drivers

If you know what motivates you, it will be easier to make decisions about the direction you want your life to take, and then stay on track. The deeper those motivators, the stronger your decisions and actions will be. For maximum power, go as deep as you can, all the way to the fundamental core values that drive you.

You can reverse-engineer this process. Using the vision of your ultimate goal – the incredible life you're building for yourself – ask yourself 'So what?'[9] For every response, ask again.

---

[8] As quoted in Haruki Murakami, *Novelist as a Vocation*.

[9] This is similar to the 'Five Whys' or 'Seven Whys' approach that you may be familiar with. It's become such a commonplace tool that it is hard to say for certain who invented it, but seems to have originated with 大野耐一 (or Taiichi Ohno as he's also known), at Toyota in the mid-Twentieth century. Our version changes the question, from 'Why?' to 'So what?' which has a subtle effect on the form your responses take. 'So what?' is deliberately confrontational and forces you to consider your motivations in the face of naysaying provocation. Getting good at asking this question will help you overcome negative comments that risk getting in the way of you achieving your goals - whether those comments are made by other people, or come from your own self-doubt.

Keep going. Imagine you are having a conversation with a persistent toddler. Around half a dozen cycles seems to work well, but it might take you more or fewer: that's OK. As with almost every task in this book, it works best with a pen or pencil and a sheet of paper, so you can see the process happen in front of you. You'll know you've got to the end when the responses have reached the emotions level. You can then put a line through all, but the first and last stage. This directly links the goal you want to the values that drive it, and makes a powerful mission statement.

Please read the following example with an open mind, because we don't want to accidentally influence you into an inaccurate personal response. For example, a toddler interrogating someone who says they want to open a donkey sanctuary might produce the following sequence of answers:

1. Because I want to help ill-treated donkeys.
2. Because I think it's awful that some donkeys are ill-treated.
3. Because I love donkeys.
4. Because I love all animals.
5. Because I love every single living thing on this planet.
6. Because I feel a deep connection with all life-forms.
7. Because all life is sacred to me.

Cut out the middle bits and you get:

- I will open a donkey sanctuary because all life is sacred to me.

WHAM! That is a punchy mission statement.

Now you know your core values, you have a compass point to follow to keep you on track. You can now start to define and build your strategy for success. Not just success in achieving the goals, but success in living according to your values.

Because your strategy will be based on your values (rather than specific goals), it won't be detrimental to your happiness should the precise nature of your goals change over time. You may realise there is another way of living your life in alignment with your values that you had not been aware of before. As well as donkeys, you might decide to help camels. If that's the case, you don't need to be afraid of changing your goals as you know you'll be doing so for the right reasons.

Ikigai

The Japanese concept *ikigai* (生き甲斐) refers to something that gives a person a reason for living, their purpose. It is a motivating force, or something that brings deep fulfilment. The pleasure that comes from achieving or doing something you're passionate about.

Clearly, cultivating *ikigai* will help you on your journey to an incredible life. Find your sense of purpose and values, then work in alignment with those values. This is why the exercises around your values and intrinsic goals are so important.

To convert this into a useful tool, rather than just a point of interest, take your values and match them up to the things you are good at or interested in. Write your values down one side of a page, and your skills down the other, then draw lines linking the two. These are the activities you can do to work according to your values. Take those, and identify which ones are useful to others (and that they're willing to pay for!). These are a solid foundation upon which to build a career or business.

Visit https://www.govlm.com/free-resources/ - the free resources page on our website - to download an interpretation of the *ikigai* model which explores what actions you can take to fulfil your purpose. It addresses what you love, what you are good at, what the world needs and what you are paid for. Then actionable steps can be applied.

You have gifts and talents (your superpowers) that correspond to your values. If you can be paid to use those talents, the work you do will feel less like a chore and more like a source of joy.

Why do you do what you do?

Similar to the 'So what?' tool is the 'How did that happen?' tool. This follows the same process, of sequentially repeating a question, but is designed to help you evaluate why you've done certain things and how you've ended up in particular situations. By asking 'How did that happen?' you can establish the motivations behind your actions and lifestyle. It's a useful task to do because it may identify traps you've previously fallen into, that you are in danger of falling into again. Traps such as automatic reactions, lazy assumptions, or following a narrative that others have written for you.; the kind of thing that can lead you to act in ways that aren't true to your deep values. By focusing this task on negative or unwanted actions, you can pin-point the causes and work out why it is that you do the things you'd rather not do.

Alternatively, focus on the decisions that led to a happy event, and it may identify positive motivators that you want to carry with you in this next stage of your life.

So ask yourself: how did that happen?

How did you get here?

Look at the key decisions that have led to your current career and lifestyle. From school (Which subjects should I take?), through to your personal life (Where shall I live? Who should I be in a relationship with?), to work (What job should I accept?), and beyond. Jot them down, ask 'how did that happen?' and see if you can classify each as being a 'good' decision, or a 'less good' decision. We're not going to say 'bad', as we're all about positivity and there's always a lesson to be learned. What, if anything, do the good decisions have in common? How about the 'less good' ones? If there are trends or patterns, you may be able to work out why you made the choices you did. This can help you make future decisions in a more self-aware manner.

Don't beat yourself up if you've found yourself in a situation that isn't the one you wanted. This process isn't about admonishment or self-criticism, but understanding. We want you to recognise and appreciate the steps you have already taken so that you can take your next steps, and make your future decisions, armed with better information about yourself.

Your previous decisions may well have been the correct ones at the time. People change. What we want changes. The world around us changes, and opportunities come and go. If you've spent years pursuing a particular career path, please don't view it as being a waste of your time, effort, or training should you decide to change direction and do something else. It's your career and you can do what you want with it. Instead, recognise the benefits of your experience to date.

> After I finished my degree, I just wanted to have a break from the creative space and had a wonderful opportunity to fly as a cabin crew member. I did the ground school and flung myself down a slide and learned all the drills and everything. Then I did my cabin management training as well, which was great. During that time I had the most fantastic experiences, made lifelong friends, and learned so much about human nature.
> – Tracy Fryer, Director at Design Studio Perth (Perth, Western Australia)

Investigate your opinions

We've asked you to go deep and question your motivations, goals, personality type, and relationships. We'll also ask you to question your opinions. This isn't necessarily something you can do now, as you might not have something burning away to confront. Rather, bear this exercise in mind the next time you find yourself feeling strongly for or against something, someone, or a course of action.

Why have you taken a dislike to a particular person? Why do you feel so strongly about building your website in-house? Why do you prefer the art of Picasso to Monet?

The opinion doesn't matter: it's the questioning that counts. By exploring the reasons why we instinctively feel or act a certain way, we can understand our motivations, hopes, or fears. This can help us get better at *responding* with intention, rather than *reacting* automatically. Don't do it for every single little thing or you'll never get anything done. But every now and then, if something big comes along, slow down, take a moment, and investigate your opinion. The answers may take some thought, or you could find they're fairly straightforward.

To practise, start by asking yourself why you like or dislike this book? If you've read this far, but you're not a fan, that's OK. Our egos are strong enough to handle the criticism and we are comfortable in the knowledge that we have written this based on *our* truth. That might not be your truth, so it may not resonate with you. If so, attempt to understand why. Likewise, if you love this book, try and understand why that is the case. Either way, the answers may be helpful to you.

What qualities do you admire in others?

We're going to be straight with you and explain the mechanics of this question. We humans seem to have a tendency to be hard on ourselves. We struggle to think of things about ourselves that we like, but can easily come up with a whole list of things we would want to change. So there really isn't much point in us telling you to think about your negative points, because:

a.   It's not a very nice way to think about yourself, and we'd rather you were more positive.

b.   You probably do it anyway, without us asking.

There's also not much point in us telling you *not* to do it, either, as they're the kind of thoughts that can creep in whether we want them to or not.

Instead, we would like you to make a list of the qualities you most admire in other people you know. Think of people you admire, or who you are close to, and jot down what it is about them that you like.

Once you've completed your list, look at the qualities you've written down. Are those qualities you have, too? Even just a little bit? If so, give yourself a pat on the back. If they're qualities you do not have, but would like, you can also give yourself a pat on the back. Why? Because you've just identified areas to work on which are going to help you become more like the people you admire.

Growth and fixed mindsets

Having a growth mindset is essential for success.[10] A growth mindset is where you look at opportunities with a willingness to explore new ideas and fresh ways of thinking. It's fluid and expansive. This is opposed to a fixed mindset, which limits you to doing what you already know and are comfortable with. It's static and constrained.

Having a growth mindset gives you the freedom to operate in new ways and explore new possibilities. Adopting or cultivating a growth mindset is the first step to building your launch pad to achieve escape velocity.

A fixed mindset is not just limiting, but more fragile. New ideas, or things not going as expected, present as challenges or problems. This can lead to a mental disconnect between expectations and reality that can result in feelings of failure or an unwillingness to take on challenges. It's a slippery slope that can lead to an avoidance of criticism and a self-perception that one cannot change, so therefore shouldn't even try.

Switch to a growth mindset and problems or unexpected events become opportunities. Pessimism gives way to optimism, and, as disability rights advocate, Helen Keller, said, 'Optimism is the faith that leads to achievement.' Criticism is something to learn from. New ideas are exciting, not intimidating. Other people's opinions become stimulating and their examples inspiring.

---

[10] The term 'growth mindset' was explained by Stanford University Psychologist, Carol Dwek in *Mindset: How to Fulfil Your Potential*, Robinson, 2012.

If you're stuck in a situation you want to get out of, or you wish to build and sustain a business, you've got to embrace the wonderful uncertainty of a growth mindset, no matter how uncomfortable it might seem at first.

Entrepreneurial Mindset Profile®

Vicki is a Master Trainer of the Entrepreneurial Mindset Profile® (EMP), a cutting-edge assessment tool which examines the skills and capabilities that are needed to identify and leverage your entrepreneurial mindset for personal competitive edge. Developing an entrepreneurial mindset can help you make the most of opportunities, learn from setbacks and build further resilience.

The EMP was devised by Mark Davis, Jennifer Hall and Pam Mayer at Eckerd College's Leadership Development Institute, in the USA. It's a validated and reliable psychometric tool, reinforced by academic research, and supported by partners including universities across the world, Institute Workplace Dynamics in Paris, Institute for Leadership Dynamics in Germany, MoneyMind in Brazil, and WeBC in Canada.

Davis, Hall and Mayer identified seven key personality traits and seven skills relating to entrepreneurship. They defined a series of scales to measure them, and mapped where successful entrepreneurs and corporate managers scored against those scales. The personality scales are:

- Independence.
- Preference for limited structure.
- Nonconformity.
- Risk acceptance.
- Action orientation.
- Passion.
- Need to achieve.

The skills scales are:

- Future focus.
- Idea generation.
- Execution.
- Self-confidence.
- Optimism.
- Persistence.
- Interpersonal sensitivity.

They then created an assessment tool, based on a series of questions relating to each of the personality and skills scales, to measure how participants compared to the benchmarks they had established. Completing the EMP assessment is a straightforward multiple-choice exercise, with no trick questions or essays required. It's not stressful to do and only takes a few moments.

The tool is nuanced - it's not just a case of hitting the max score on each item to have a more developed entrepreneurial mindset, nor will it tell you if you should become an entrepreneur - as it is the interplay between the different personality and skills scales, and one's context that is important. The EMP assessment is all about recognising and developing an entrepreneurial mindset.

Completing the questionnaire is something you can do yourself. Helping you make sense of the results is where Vicki, as an accredited EMP Master Trainer, comes in. Vicki has been trained by Eckerd College to interpret the results, provide insights as to what they mean, and work with you to develop ideas you can put into practice.

The process is pain-free and you'll come out of it feeling enthused, with a greater understanding of what makes you tick and what to do in order to thrive. Don't just take Vicki's word for it. Here's what Jonathan thought of the EMP process when he went through it:

> As a writer who also works with charities, I suspect I'm not a typical subject for the EMP. I'm not heading up a tech start-up or managing teams of people in The City, and I don't have any ambition to be the next Jeff Bezos (I'm quite happy here on Earth, thank you very much). However, I am a business owner - even if it's just a one-man band, freelance sole trader business - and it is important to me that my business is successful.
>
> Amongst the things I have to consider, to achieve my professional goals, are attracting and retaining customers, developing and selling products, and exploring how to grow my business. These all require me to adopt and maintain an entrepreneurial mindset.

As such, I was keen to take the EMP assessment and discuss the findings with Vicki.

Answering the questions was easy. It took just a few minutes of my time, using an online portal. The questions are all about you, the person completing the EMP assessment, so this is one assessment where you'll definitely know all the answers.

After the online questions, I had a conversation with Vicki to talk through my responses. In general, the assessment didn't reveal any great surprises, as I tend to be well-tuned into myself, but it was interesting to see how my scores compared to the benchmarks. In some areas (e.g. idea generation, interpersonal sensitivity, and nonconformity), I was reassured to see my scores were similar to those of a typical successful entrepreneur. In others (e.g. risk acceptance, action orientation, and execution), I deviated far below the curve.

This is helpful information to have. I may have plenty of ideas, but if I'm not willing to take a risk and make them happen, I'm stifling the potential for growth. Vicki gave me ideas of things I can do to improve in this regard, with clear steps to take. I have since cultivated a shift in my approach to new opportunities which quickly led to exciting new projects.

As I was intrigued by the EMP scales, Vicki and I talked about other scenarios in which the scores might not interact in the way you'd initially suspect. For example, being a hard worker, conscientious, and good with people are all positive traits you may assume to be a likely indicator of success. But without self-awareness and understanding, they can easily lead to doing too much, for as many people as possible, to an excessively high standard, and burning out in the process. Completing the EMP can help avoid such pitfalls.

I am not someone who enjoys being the subject of assessment. Reviews, appraisals, and even receiving positive feedback make me feel uncomfortable, so I avoid these scenarios. I'll admit to being a little nervous going into the EMP process, but I needn't have been as it was a constructive, positive process.

Whether you have entrepreneurial ambitions or not, developing a better understanding of your personality and skills is a valuable route to self-improvement and success in your professional (and social) life. After all, you've got to know yourself to grow yourself.

Reflection

You can achieve an incredible life by reflecting on your mindset. This can be hard to do when you're in a state of panic or flux. If your head is bursting with the stress of everything you need to do, or stuck in fight, flight, or freeze mode, you don't have the mental capacity to think effectively. Slow down. Stop. Breathe.

Meditation and meditative practices give you the time and mental space to explore your inner world and get to know yourself. If you're not a fan of yoga mats and incense, going for a long walk on your own can do the job. This is something worth coming back to often, as your vision, values and mission may evolve in time. As we get older, we gain more life experience, and the people and environment around us change. Therefore it's understandable that our inner world can shape-shift to accommodate that. Re-exploring your inner world regularly can help keep you on the track that's right for you.

The Gandhi quote at the beginning of this part of the book summarises why this process is so important. Our beliefs influence how we think. In turn, our thoughts lead to our words, which lead to our actions, which determine the life we build for ourselves. Given this direct link from our beliefs to our destiny, it is clearly vital to understand those beliefs before we begin to act. Otherwise we run the risk of doing an awful lot of action and not getting the result we want. This is why we ask you to slow down, breathe and meditate – to look at your inner world and be crystal clear about who you are, what you believe, and what you want.

'But I don't have time for that!' you say.

To which we say, 'No-one else can do your self-reflection for you. If you don't do it, it won't happen. If you're happy with your stressed-out state, then carry on as you are. But if you want to change, you're going to have to put the work in.'

As a starting point, put a note in your calendar on a day within the next week (because we don't want this to drag on any longer) and block out a few minutes (as many as you can spare) for self-reflection. This time is sacred, protected. Don't let anything or anyone else take that block of time from you. Sit and think. If you're still stuck at the beginning of your momentum mindset journey, start with the first exercise in this book. If you're part-way along, pick things up at the most appropriate point for you. When you've completed your block of allotted time, jump back into the rushing blur of life stress if that's what you need to do, but we would wager that your heart will feel a little lighter for having taken the time to slow down and give some time back to yourself. This little glimpse of an incredible life can be the motivation to find another block of time to keep working on your plan to achieve escape velocity. Schedule a recurring meeting with yourself. Keep it up and it will get easier each time. Eventually, you'll be flying.

This process of self-reflection is of vital importance because it will show you how to achieve your dreams. The ability to understand what makes you tick, and to recognise what you are best at, are two of the most powerful tools you can have. Grasp those and you can do great things. The key to maximising your positive impact, on your own life and that of others, can be summarised as:

- Key drivers + Superpowers = Maximum positive impact

That's because this combination makes the most of your motivation to do something and your ability to do it. Combine these two factors and you give yourself the best chance of achieving escape velocity. If you don't make the most of these, it'll be like striding forwards in shoes that don't fit, to a destination you don't care about. That will require a lot more work than is necessary and be deeply unsatisfying. We don't want you to do that. Take the time to understand yourself. Don't do more, do better.

Self-

There are a lot of 'self' words to understand when on a journey of self-improvement. This is a good spot to discuss them, as the language we use can help improve our mindset. We've just mentioned one of these 'self' words, two sentences ago: self-improvement. This is the process of making changes in your life – to what you do, how you approach problems and opportunities, training you undertake, the habits you cultivate, and more – with the goal of having a positive effect. This book, taking you from a state of stationary inertia to an incredible life, is a self-improvement book. In this instance, 'self' refers to both the intended beneficiary of the work and the person doing it.

Other 'self' words that will be affected by your process of self-improvement include self-confidence, self-belief, self-drive, self-determination, self-worth, self-compassion, and self-esteem. These are all factors recognised as necessary to create a life in which we can feel happy: confidence in our own abilities, belief that we can do it, the drive to get things done, determining our own course of action, recognising our own value, being kind to oneself, and respecting and admiring oneself.

This last factor, self-esteem, can be problematic, however. Consider the view of academic and author, Kristin Neff:[11]

> Self-esteem is a judgement of self-worth. It's like a judgement that 'I'm a good person' or 'I'm a bad person' or 'I'm somewhere in-between.' And it really focuses on kind of the worst of the self.

If your self-esteem is low, it can be hard to feel like you deserve to improve your life. If this is the case, self-compassion is vitally important. It's probably the most important 'self' of all, because without it you will be unable to forgive yourself for past actions, understand the circumstances that led to them, and take positive steps forward. Neff, again:

> It's a matter of treating yourself with kindness, care and support, the way you would treat a good friend. So even when you feel you've done something badly, or you aren't feeling so good about yourself, you're accepting and kind to yourself.

It's about having a caring, sympathetic emotional attitude to yourself. Be warm towards yourself when encountering pain and personal shortcomings. Don't ignore the situation or, worse still, hurt yourself with self-criticism. Be your own wise friend who

---

[11] Kristin Neff is Associate Professor Human Development and Culture, Educational Psychology Department, University of Texas at Austin and author of *Self-Compassion: The Proven Power of Being Kind to Yourself*, Hodder & Stoughton, 2011.

puts an arm around your shoulders when you fall, pulls you deep into their embrace and says, 'Well, what happened there?' before wiping away your tears, whispering words of encouragement into your ear, and pushing you back out into the world.

It starts within

To emerge from a state of inertia, to progress toward an incredible life, you need to know yourself. We can be certain the most successful people in the world have worked on themselves. You should too.

Look within. Understand your mindset and recognise what makes you tick by asking self-reflective questions. Look back to when you were a child. Do you remember what you wanted to be when you grew up? What made you feel a sense of purpose? What were your natural talents and abilities? What activities and roles did you enjoy? Which didn't you enjoy? When did you feel most satisfied? Then go big: What are you meant to do in the world?

To help answer this massive, scary question, identify your values. We are all unique with our own core set of values and beliefs. It is important to establish what yours are, to define your mission. Then you can build a strategy for success that is right for you.

We've talked already about how achieving intrinsic goals leads to a greater, longer-lasting, deeper satisfaction than if we achieve extrinsic goals. Success that is related to our internal, core values is always going to feel sweeter than ticking a box someone else has decided is important.

Likewise, intrinsic motivational factors will always be stronger than extrinsic motivators. You will always have more willingness to do something you truly want to do, than something someone else tells you to do. Of course extrinsic motivators can still be powerful. Someone else cracking the whip will always get you moving. However, if you can find a way of getting yourself moving – without someone else forcing you to do it – you stand a much improved chance of reaching your goals.

For this reason, it is so important you start this journey to get unstuck and achieve escape velocity yourself. Don't do it because someone else said you should, or because you want to achieve another person's definition of success. Do it because you want to, and do it on your own terms, in your own way. Not only will you improve your chances of success, but the end result will taste all the sweeter for it.

CHAPTER FOUR

Why are you stuck?

If you change the way you look at things, the things you look at change.

> – Wayne Dyer, author and therapist

Audit

Doing a life audit involves taking a comprehensive and holistic approach to your life, identifying areas that may be out of alignment with your values and goals, and developing strategies to create a more fulfilling and purpose-driven life.

Let's carry out a quick audit of your current situation. How would you mark yourself out of 10 in the following four areas? 0 is poor, 10 is as good as it gets. Here are some key components of a life audit and what they involve:

- **Physical**: assessing your physical health, including your diet, exercise habits, and overall wellness. It may involve developing a fitness plan, seeking medical attention for any health concerns, or incorporating mindfulness practices into your daily routine.

- **Emotional**: assessing your emotional well-being, including your relationships, mental health, and overall happiness. It also involves identifying any emotional challenges you may be facing, such as stress, anxiety, or depression, and developing strategies to address them, such as seeking therapy or practising self-care.

- **Spiritual**: assessing your spiritual well-being and connection to a higher power or purpose. It may involve evaluating your religious beliefs, meditation or mindfulness practices, or other forms of spiritual connection.

- **Financial**: assessing your financial situation, including your income, expenses, savings, and debt. It also involves evaluating your financial goals and identifying steps you can take to achieve them, such as creating a budget, reducing expenses, or increasing income.

- **Career**: assessing your professional life, including your job satisfaction, career goals, and work-life balance. It may involve identifying your strengths and weaknesses, exploring new career opportunities, or developing strategies to advance in your current field.

Add your scores together to find your total out of 50. What does the spread of your points look like? Is one area outscoring the others and artificially inflating your overall score? Or is there an area that is dragging you down? This quick exercise can tell you how to distribute your energy and focus.

To get the most benefit from this exercise, you need to repeat it regularly. This should flag up anything that needs addressing. Every 90 days will do, but you can choose the interval that suits you. Pop it in your calendar as a recurring item, blocking out the time so it remains a priority and doesn't get bumped down your to-do list. Over time, you can track your progress. Hopefully the results will improve, which will provide a confidence boost and reassurance that you're doing the right thing. If they start slipping down, then at least you'll be able to spot this, arrest the decline, and refocus on lifting yourself back up again.

Look forward

The past. The present. The future. They're rarely three distinct phases, as your past memories and future dreams can all overlap with your present state, as time keeps ticking on. A certain amount of reflection on the past is an essential part of becoming unstuck (and something we've already covered), but it is important not to linger on the past any longer than necessary. If you continually focus on the past you may not leave room in the future for new things which can make your life better.

Exorcise your past demons by writing down all the things you want to leave behind: behaviours, bad memories, and bullsh*t stories about yourself (told *to* you, or *by* you). Write them down, take a moment to acknowledge the lessons you've learned, then destroy the list. Put it in a fire, run it through a shredder, rip it up and leave it in the cat's litter tray. Whatever. You can do it with as much or as little ceremony as you want. It doesn't matter how you do it because, frankly, this is a symbolic act. Unless you've got serious shaman skills, you probably aren't going to successfully delete your actual memories. But the sensory experience of committing the act of destruction is important.

When you find yourself negatively ruminating on the past, close your eyes and remember what it felt like to write out your list and destroy it. Remember the movement of your hands, the spark of the match, the smell of the smoke, the sight of your cat defecating on it. The more vivid and visceral the better. Remember the act and rededicate yourself to forward progression along your chosen path.

Think about all the future events you're looking forward to, or are feeling excited about. Again, don't just think about it, but write them down: A list of ten positive things that appear in your future. Next to them, write down why you're looking forward to them. This is about conscious consideration and full appreciation, not just automatic action. Why are you so excited about the concert next month? Why are you looking forward to brunch with your best friend? Why can't you wait to go on that course? Repeat this process every 90 days and keep a record as a future reminder of all the great things that you've enjoyed.

If you're reading this and thinking, 'But there's nothing I'm looking forward to,' that is a massive red flag and you need to correct that situation right now. You must always have stuff to look forward to. Yes, life is hectic and you may have financial pressures to worry about, but that is precisely why you have to find things to get excited about. They don't need to be expensive, spectacular, or look good on Instagram. They can be simple, low key and personal. Look up events happening in your town, phone up an old friend, block off a few hours in your calendar to go for a walk in the park. Whatever you do, please make sure you always have a minimum of three things per month you're looking forward to, and that you will feel grateful for after they've occurred.

Live with an eye to the future, while making the most of the present, and feelings of hope, aspiration, and joy will permeate through your being. It will influence how you think and how you hold yourself. It will have an effect on your interactions with others and the way you make decisions in your business and personal life. People will start to notice the difference. You will notice the difference.

What are you afraid of?

The path from a state of being stuck to achieving escape velocity can be tough. Undoing the shackles that have held you back, and building a new life, is going to involve some hard choices and some hard work. There may be times when you are stressed out and afraid that you're not doing the right thing. Those times aren't fun, but they are natural, and they can be made easier by acknowledging those emotions. Don't suppress your feelings. Don't be afraid of talking about them. Find a confidante you trust, and talk to them. Be vulnerable.

The author, DBC Pierre, has this advice for writers: 'What would you write if you weren't afraid? Write that.'[12] Substitute writing for whatever it is you do, and the advice still holds true. Lose the fear and your true self can flourish.

What is it that you're afraid of? Identifying your fears can be a growth opportunity. If you find your fears, you can address them. If you're afraid of failure, work on overcoming that. If you're afraid of people laughing at you, work on overcoming that. If you're afraid of loneliness, work on overcoming that. If there are things that trigger unwelcome emotions or memories, address them so they lose their power over you.

You might be able to face your fears alone, or it may take the skills of a professional therapist or counsellor. Whatever it takes, you'll feel better for doing so. A head full of fears has no space for dreams. By liberating yourself from your fears, you'll have the freedom to stride towards your goals.

Bravery

'Anxiety is the dizziness of freedom.' So wrote the philosopher, Soren Kierkegaard, discussing the uncertain, uncomfortable feeling that can arise when we have too many possibilities to comprehend. Though we long for freedom and autonomy, we are also reassured by familiar structures and a sense of belonging

---

[12] DBC Pierre, *Release the Bats*, Faber & Faber, 2016.

to a community. As with most things, the middle ground is where we would like to be. Not too much freedom, as that is unnerving and can be lonely, but enough to have some control over our lives. This is a useful thing to recognise and remind yourself of for two reasons:

1. If you're feeling anxious, that may be because you have achieved a level of autonomy and freedom you're not used to. If this is part of your plan to live an incredible life, then celebrate this anxiety. It means you're on the right path!

2. But, if you're feeling *too* anxious about a decision, you may be able to rein this in by cutting some of the options and narrowing the range of possibilities. Too many menu items? Just look at the vegetarian dishes and you'll cut out most of the choices. Not enough structure in your working day? Define some working hours and pop them on your calendar.

Still scared? Do it anyway. Bryn Walbrook is a former planner at top branding and advertising agencies who became an entrepreneur with a start-up sustainable beauty brand. This is his view on the choice between making a decision based on fear, or making a decision based on bravery:

> Why on earth would you ever make a decision based on fear? There's only ever one choice, and it's the brave one, right? The brave choice might be harder in the short term, but it's more beneficial in the long term.

We couldn't agree more. If you want long term positive progress, sometimes you're going to have to get uncomfortable and do hard things.

The futility of worrying

Nina Fraser is an artist who lives in Lisbon. She has a wonderful, open way of thinking about life events, both positive and negative. This was especially useful when she had to deal with one of the worst situations you can find yourself in: your home being destroyed by a gas explosion. In one moment, Nina and Paulo (her partner) lost everything. What they did next is a remarkable story of resilience and rebuilding, but it isn't our story to tell. Instead, we want to pass on a nugget of wisdom that Nina shared with Jonathan recently, which makes perfect, logical sense.

It's not worth worrying now about a situation you may have to deal with in the future. That's because by the time it happens (that's if it even does happen), you will be different (with new knowledge, experience, or ideas), and the world around you will be different (changing the context in which this situation occurs). So any worried planning that you did in the past will be out-of-date and potentially ineffective. Therefore, there's no point in worrying about something until it happens.

The hutch mentality

Jonathan's aunt, uncle and cousins used to have a rabbit called Badger. He was black and white, with no ears due to a birth defect. He was anti-social and not a fan of the hutch he was given, so he moved out. He dug a burrow (sett may be more appropriate in his case) and was rarely seen by the family, only emerging to eat the food left out for him.

We're going to use the example of Badger as a way to explore the hutch mentality, its potential pitfalls, and the opportunities that come from understanding and reframing it and ourselves.

Typically, domestic rabbits seem happy to live in the hutches or cages we give them and are quite content to be looked after. Consider house rabbits: They live in an environment far removed from their natural habitat, yet don't tend to run out of the front door when the opportunity presents itself.

One possible explanation for this is that as a small prey animal, with big ears and wide-set eyes to look out for danger, rabbits feel safe and secure in a sociable, protected environment. Instead of the hutch being a confining environment that keeps them trapped in, it's a protective environment that keeps threats out.

An alternative explanation is that domesticated rabbits have become conditioned to captivity. They don't know anything else, have no concept of what life might be like in the wild and are blissfully, ignorantly content to remain caged by their owners.

We don't know which option is true for rabbits. For humans, however, we're inclined to think both can be correct. What's more, they can be correct in the same person, at the same time, depending on the area of life being considered, with positive and negative side-effects.

It would be easy to think, 'Humans are intelligent, so we know when we're being trapped'. That may be true in clear cases of restricted liberty, such as being imprisoned, but what about less obvious, subtle circumstances? For example:

- The person who has no control over their own life because of the coercive behaviour of an abusive partner.
- The working class boy from a former mining town who wants to be a ballet dancer, but is told 'Boys don't dance.'
- The person who doesn't pursue their career dreams because they're comfortable with the easy, familiar role they currently have.

Clearly, these hutches aren't all alike. The first is horrible manipulation; the second is restrictive social conditioning; and the third could be considered quite a nice situation to find yourself in if your career isn't the most important thing in the world to you. There are four steps to breaking free from your hutch:

1. Recognising you're in a hutch.
2. Deciding if you actually want to change your situation.
3. Planning your escape.

4.   Putting the plan into action.

Thinking about hamsters, rather than rabbits, for a moment, they appear to be 'all-or-nothing' in their approach to life with a high, nervous energy. They're either hidden away, sleeping for hours, or running flat out on their wheels. They're putting in a lot of work, but not going anywhere. Why is this?

Anyone who has pulled up floorboards searching for a pet hamster that has gotten free, will likely agree that hamsters seem to have an urge to escape. This could be from an instinctive understanding the cage is not their natural environment. Yet without direct experience or knowledge of the outside world a hamster is not going to know where to go, how to get there, or even how to survive.

Again, this can apply to humans. You may have a feeling your current circumstances are not the best environment for you. You may even be putting in a lot of energy trying to escape from those circumstances, or attempting to change that environment. Without a clear sense of direction or an understanding of what you need to do to move on and thrive, you run the risk of getting stuck on the treadmill (putting in a lot of effort and getting nothing in return) or disappearing under the floorboards (making a change, but not the right one).

To a degree, this is an inevitable challenge that has to be overcome. Any new venture, or big life decision, is a leap into the unknown. That can't be avoided entirely, but the risk of failure can be reduced.

Known-unknowns (the gaps in your knowledge that you're aware of) can be filled in with research and training. The unknown-unknowns (the gaps in your knowledge that you don't know about) are trickier, but there will almost certainly be someone out there who can help make you aware of the things you didn't even know you needed to think about. This is where the guiding hand of a trusted friend, loved one, colleague, mentor or coach can make your path clearer. Even with support, it can still be scary. The most important steps in life often are.

Taking a simplified, somewhat altered version of Plato's cave analogy, imagine you've been confined to a cave for your whole life and have only ever seen pictures of the outside world. One day, you're given the opportunity to leave the cave, but the light of the sun is so blinding you want to retreat back to the comforting familiarity of the darkness. Stick it out and let your eyes adjust, however, and you'll be able to enjoy the sights and sensations of a whole world you didn't know was out there.

It's hard to achieve this on your own. A good team or coach can support you to get through the overwhelming blinding light stage. This is why it's so important to surround yourself with the right people, whether they provide practical, financial, or emotional support.

The strategies above assume you need to leave your hutch for good, but that might not always be the case. It's also important to recognise there are instances when it's more than OK to stay in your hutch, or to come and go depending on the conditions. As long as it's not holding you back, a hutch can provide you with the tools to get out there and achieve great things.

If your current hutch doesn't help you, seek out a new one, or work to improve the one you have. Unless you are trapped against your will, you hold the keys to your hutch. If you want it to be, you can make your hutch a home, not a cage.

There is absolutely nothing wrong with cultivating an environment that provides comfort, safety and security. Indeed, we'd recommend it. It could be a physical safe space, the support of others, or even a mindset you cultivate within yourself.

To Jonathan's mind, that's what Badger did. He may have moved out of his hutch, seeking freedom, but he didn't venture too far. Every day he emerged from his tunnel for fresh air and to eat the food left out for him in an area of the garden he knew to be safe. With his essential needs met, he could focus on his life's work: tunnelling under the garage.

Viewed through this lens, a hutch isn't always a negative place to find yourself. Provided it isn't a prison or a cage, it can be a mental or physical refuelling or repair station. Or better yet, it can be a launch pad. A base from which you plan and prepare before taking off, escaping the gravitational pull of everything that holds you back, to soar higher than you ever dared to dream was possible.

Pain points

In literature, TV, films, and anything where a strong, dramatic story is required, the Hero's Journey is a solid way to structure a narrative. Typically, the Hero's Journey follows this pattern:

- The hero experiences a call to head off on an adventure.

- They leave the comfortable, known world and travel into the unknown.
- They may benefit from the help of others.
- There will be challenges and temptations.
- At some point, everything will appear lost, but they'll overcome this ultimate struggle.
- This experience will transform them.
- Past issues will be resolved.
- They'll achieve their goals.
- And finally settle back into a comfortable, known state of equilibrium, enjoying the benefits of their efforts.

This is exciting and makes for a good story, which is why it pops up everywhere from classical Greek mythology through to contemporary fiction. It's basically *The Lord of the Rings*. But it's a stressful way to live in the real world. It would be quite nice not to have so many challenges and temptations, or need to come close to death in a fiery volcano, for example, in order to grow.

That's not always something we can control, of course. As much as we would prefer your personal Hero's Journey to be a pleasurable, relaxing affair, the reality is there will be challenges to overcome. Accept there is a possibility you will struggle, and do what you can to learn and grow from the tough times.

You will already have a great deal of resilience within you, even if you haven't realised it yet. To demonstrate this to yourself, think back to a time in your life where you experienced a setback or significant problem. Then, write down the lessons you learned as a result. There's a chance some of them will be negatively-framed ('Don't walk through swamps full of ghosts'), but positively-framed lessons will be more powerful ('I can trust Sam with my life,' or 'I can do more than I thought possible').

Carrying out this exercise will allow you to demonstrate to yourself that you have the resilience to deal with setbacks and have grown stronger from those experiences. Setbacks are part of life, but so are comebacks, and they feel great.

Forgive yourself, then move on

There's a lot of good habits we can adopt in the pursuit of living an intentional, mindful life with the goal of achieving our dreams. Eating well, sleeping well, journalling, meditating, exercising, seeing friends, spending time in nature, engaging with our community, and so on. What's often left off the list is balancing consistency and the cultivation of good habits, with the need to take it easy and cut yourself some slack now and then.

When you're already stressed by the thought of all the things you have to do, adding new items to your to-do list runs the risk of making you more stressed; even if those additional stressors are meant to be stress-relieving.

Be kind to yourself, display some self-compassion, and switch how you view them. It's not a list of things you *have* to do, but a list of things you would *like* to do, and have *chosen* to do. Doing everything on the list is not a minimum requirement for success.

Consider a list with ten items on it. If you're currently doing none of them regularly, then one or two per day is still an improvement and represents growth. There'll be good days when you might even complete the list, and bad days when you do nothing. What's important is that over time they average out in a positive way. Some of those actions will gradually become habits and your benchmark will shift its way upwards from zero, to one, to two, and so on.

This is a much more sustainable approach than attempting to achieve all ten items from day one. It requires you to forgive yourself when your day hasn't gone to plan, consider the reasons why (so you can learn from the experience), and move on. One day, you may even find yourself achieving all the items on your idealised to-do list, without even realising that you're doing it.

Roadblocks

As the saying goes, 'Every level has another devil'. It is not always the case that the further you progress on your journey to escape velocity, the easier it gets. Even if life starts to get smoother for you, or you're working more in alignment with your values, there will inevitably be something that pops up for you to deal with. Your sense of purpose and direction will give you the strength to overcome the new devils that appear when you reach a new stage of your life.

There will be external problems you can't avoid, so make

your life easier by minimising the number of devils you create for yourself. The road is tough enough as it is: don't self-sabotage and put up unnecessary roadblocks. And if something unexpected prevents you from moving forward, adopt the singer Cher's philosophy: 'If you can't go straight ahead, you just go around the corner.'

Imposter syndrome

The inability to believe that we're deserving of our own success, or the sense that we're insufficiently or illegitimately qualified for the position we find ourselves is known as imposter syndrome.[13] It is one of the biggest unnecessary roadblocks we can put in our own way. Yet it is a stubborn roadblock to get rid of. Reassure yourself with the knowledge that it is a common affliction. Almost all of the people you look up to will have experienced imposter syndrome at some point. That said, you don't have to live with it all the time. There are three things you can do to address it:

1. Remind yourself of your self-worth. Silence the voice that tells you you're not good enough by drowning it out with positive affirmations. You do deserve success. You do have the confidence to go after your dreams. You do have the right to live an incredible life.

---

[13] The work of Dr Valerie Young and the Imposter Syndrome Institute is worth looking at if you struggle to overcome imposter syndrome.

2. Celebrate your successes. Reinforce your positive affirmations by recognising your achievements. Every day, make a note of your victories. They might be big or small, professional or personal. It could be closing a deal, making your kids laugh, another day sober, or finding the strength to get out of bed. It doesn't matter. They all count.

3. Become an expert. If you know your subject well enough, you can't be an imposter. Learn, practice, repeat.

The third point is the hardest to achieve if you're starting from a point of knowledge. But we don't think you're starting from zero. If this is the life you want, we bet that you already know more than you realise. When you've been working in a particular area for a while, you'll have picked up knowledge and expertise that is 'everyday' to you and just feels obvious or second-nature. You might already be an expert or further on the path to mastery than you thought. Acknowledge what it is you already know, through a 'glass half full' lens. Then you just have to do what's necessary to fill your skill-set up to the brim.

> For me, the EMP, and seeing my low score for confidence was a huge eye opener. It was in a workshop setting and everybody else in the workshop said, 'How can you score so low when you've come in here seeming like the most confident person ever?' That was the imposter syndrome and me not having confidence in myself. I knew after the workshop that

was what I needed to work on.

Everyday, I need to feel successful. So I do something similar to a gratitude exercise where I ask myself 'What are the small successes I've had today?' Even on the worst days you have, when you're feeling absolutely crap, there's something to feel successful about on that day.

That exercise has been one of the things that has changed my mindset and changed my imposter syndrome. Everybody has it. Even the most high profile person sitting on a stage that you're looking up to will admit at some point in their life they have had imposter syndrome. You just have to embrace it and feel comfortable in the fear. Now, I love when I get that anxious feeling because I know that's me testing myself. If I don't get that anxious feeling, maybe it's time for something else.

– Caitriona Forde, Founder and Senior Consultant at caIT (Perth, Western Australia)

If you're fearful of change, competitors, or what people are going to say, just go out and investigate what it is you're fearful of. Arm yourself with knowledge so you're not fearful of it. Whether it's imposter syndrome or other things that cause you to question yourself, it all comes back to knowledge. Go out and find out about the subjects you deal with. Become the world expert on it.

Ask me anything about shaving, whether it's razors,

blades, patents, intellectual property, trademarks, competitors, direct-to-consumer, sales, or market shares. I know this stuff because I make it my business to know it.

When you know stuff and have the knowledge, you don't need to blag it. You're not posturing. When you're genuinely armed with knowledge, the imposter syndrome goes away. Because you're not an imposter, you're an expert.

– Will King, Founder of King of Shaves (London, UK)

You are creative

'I'm not creative' has to be one of the most frequently told lies there is. So many people say it, yet they're all wrong. Every single one of them. Every decision you make - even the ones you don't realise you're making - requires a degree of creativity. From the mundane - 'What shall I have for lunch?' - through to the exciting - 'Where shall we go on holiday?' - requires some element of creative thinking.

This incorrect thinking about what is or isn't creativity has arisen because the difference between creative thinking and technical ability have become muddled. Some people might not have the artistic skill to paint a photo-realistic portrait, for example, but everyone is creative. It's just that some of us have trained that part of our brain more than others, or are more tuned into their creative instincts.

The neurosurgeon, Philippe Schucht, has this advice for people who want to further develop their natural creativity:

> If your ambition is to become more creative and innovative, you should continuously expose your mind to new and challenging situations. You must lead it off the beaten track.[14]

Stimulate your mind and it will reward you with stimulating ideas.

> Creativity is not just about how artistic you are. A lot of the time, in education, we say creativity is about how well you come up with different ideas. That's less than half of what creativity is. Being creative is about unpacking or understanding a problem in a different way. Can you see the problem from another perspective? That is the key to understanding complex things without just adding more complexity to them.
> – Dr Christopher Kueh, Design Abilities Specialist
> (Perth, Western Australia)

---

[14] Philippe Schucht quoted in '12 New Year's resolutions', *Monocle*, Issue 159, 2022.

Get back on the bike

Jonathan is a fan of watching professional cycling, especially races such as the Tour de France or the tough one day events that involve cobblestones and terrible Belgian spring weather. There are some people who enjoy watching the crashes that inevitably occur when dozens of riders are pushing themselves, racing down Alpine mountain roads at speeds the TV camera motorbikes struggle to keep up with. Jonathan's not a fan of the crashes themselves (he's not a sadist, and having broken his shoulder in a bicycle crash, he knows how it feels), but loves the chase that follows if it's one of the race favourites that goes down. Provided the rider isn't too injured to carry on, the aftermath of a crash usually goes as follows: the cyclist picks themself up off the floor and looks around for their bike. If it's broken, they'll wait for a replacement from a teammate or the support car. If it's OK, they'll hop straight back on and hammer it, riding as hard as they can, until they get back to the peloton or the lead group. Once back in the pack, they can slipstream off the other riders and rest a bit, but they know that until they reach that pack, they have to get up as fast as they can and work even harder to get back to where they were.

The same is true of life and business. If you've been knocked down, get back up. Sometimes, you might need to accept that you're too injured to go on and retire from the race. If that happens, take the time to recover properly. If you're broken, stop. Get patched up by the team doctor, have a massage, eat, sleep, and prepare to race another day.

But if you're only a little bruised, get back on the bike and ride on. The rest of the race might be far up the road, but the sooner you get back to them, the sooner you can ease up again. In a cycling race with speeds well in excess of twenty miles an hour, even a minute spent on the floor can lose you a third of a mile or more. That can be a big gap to bridge on your own.

Teammates can help. They can give you a fresh bike, shout words of encouragement, or ride ahead of you, blocking the wind and sharing the effort.

You might need to take some risks, such as bunny-hopping roundabouts and speed bumps rather than riding around them. Or you might just need to sustain your maximum effort, work harder than you thought you would need to do when you woke up that morning, and get the job done.

It might hurt, but you're stronger than you think. Races have been won by people covered in bandages, with broken bones, or riding damaged bikes with flat tyres or stuck in one gear. You may not be a professional cyclist, but you can be just as tough.

Down, but not out

Sometimes, you can't get back on the bike, the road is closed, or an asteroid destroys your rocket. The old plan is ripped up and a new approach is needed. That's OK. Refer back to your values and get creative. Ask yourself, 'What would the smartest person in the world do in this situation?'

View the challenge as an opportunity. Explore it from a

new angle. Question your preconceptions. Look for the upside. Find the silver linings. Reorientate yourself, and get going.

> Embrace the challenges. For example, you might lose a big client, but that means you now have time to work on your own project.
> – Karen Dauncey, Managing Director of Blue Cherry Online Marketing (Perth, Western Australia)

Nothing ever lasts, you know. There have been many times in my career where maybe I wasn't getting on with my boss or employer, or enjoying the job. You can find yourself thinking this is how it is going to be forever, and never see the other side. But it does get better - it always does - if you take action to make it better.

Even small, simple things can help. Start by going for a walk to clear your head. Listen to music. It changes your mood and your mindset.

I know it's difficult when you're going through difficult periods of your life, and it's very hard to change your mind. But there are positives in every situation and you have to look for them. It was difficult when my dad died of cancer, but I realised I was very fortunate to have had such a loving father.

Now, I can look at every situation and ask, 'What am I learning from this?' Because whatever it is I'm going through, I know there is something I need to learn from that situation. They're gifts wrapped in sandpaper.

Clearly, redundancy was the best thing that could have happened to me. It's not something any of us ever want - to be told you're no longer wanted or the job's no longer there - but life is a series of sliding doors moments. For me, it meant I had to make a decision to try and get a new job, or be my own boss and do something.

It's important that when something negative comes at you, you decide what it is you want to do in your life.

– Will King, Founder of King of Shaves (London, UK)

It's OK to not be OK

Even an incredible life is hard, sometimes. You have to be OK with that. It is impossible to avoid all pain or difficulty. As there is nothing you can do about that fact, you should embrace it as something that enriches your life. This is the basis of acceptance and commitment therapy (ACT).

The ACT approach takes the view that pain is inevitable, so attempting to avoid or control painful experiences just prolongs the suffering and causes other problems. If something hurts, try to understand it, rather than fight it. If the pain is inevitable, fighting it just creates more pain as you add a sense of struggle on top of the initial cause of discomfort. An acceptance of the inevitability of pain means you can develop ways of living in which you react positively and remain committed to your values, even when tough times happen.[15]

This isn't about being a masochist and intentionally hurting yourself (though sometimes, deliberately seeking discomfort can be a good thing, as we grow from challenging ourselves). It's about recognising that when difficult situations occur, that are beyond your control, you are not just being presented with an opportunity to learn from them, but an opportunity to make positive decisions to act in a way that takes you closer to being the person you want to be.

You can't be perfect, so don't stress about it

While we're on the subject of acceptance, please accept the impossibility of perfection. You cannot be perfect. There may be moments of perfection, if you're lucky, but most of the time we exist in a state of imperfection.

By all means, strive to be as good as you can be, but be OK with the truth that complete perfection is never going to happen. As the saying goes, 'good enough is good enough.'

If something works, gets the job done, or makes you

---

[15] Steven C. Hayes & Spencer Smith, *Get Out of Your Mind and Into Your Life*, New Harbinger Publications, 2005.

happy, that is enough. Stressing about the 0.1% that might theoretically be improved is only going to take the shine off the 99.9% that is good.

Often, the desire for perfection is driven by an unhelpful fear of failure and an aversion to criticism. Feedback from others can be very uncomfortable, but it is important to listen to. Good advice and constructive criticism can be a tool you can use to achieve escape velocity.

Language

Jonathan's former colleague, Clarice Montero, introduced him to the idea that 'Your words are a spell you cast on yourself and others'. It's true. Words are fantastically powerful. Their effect can be large and obvious - 'I love you' - or subtle, but still strong - 'Oh...'

We've talked about the false stories about ourselves that we believe to be true. At some point we might have recognised them as false, but when repeated often enough they can change our perceptions or behaviours. By altering how we perceive or act in the world, they shift our reality. We can't expect others to say positive things about us if we don't afford ourselves the same courtesy. So scrap the unhelpful self-talk. 'I'm not good at technology. I'm fat. I'm too scatty. I'm not creative. I never finish anything.' If there's an underlying problem, deal with it, but don't reinforce it by continually perpetuating these negative messages.

Fortunately, as much as the wrong words can hinder us, the right words can help us. Avoiding the words of other people is impossible unless you become a recluse. So you're just going to have to make sure the spells you cast are of the positive variety. This includes spells on other people, as well as yourself. Consider the following three examples:

    a.   'I should do this.'
    b.   'I need to do this.'
    c.   'I want to do this.'

They're all saying much the same thing, but in very different ways. Option a.) implies an obligation; b.) implies a compulsion or non-negotiable act; and c) implies a desire or personal choice.

All are valid in the correct setting, so we won't tell you to only ever use one of them. But, use them consciously and appropriately. If you're feeling stressed about an item on your To-Do list, check how you're talking about it. Is it something you are obliged to do, compelled to do, or choose to do? Get in the habit of picking your words with intention and you can retrain how you think.

Sorry

Are you always apologising? Don't. At least, not unless you *really* should.

Jonathan's Ukrainian friend, Valentyn, upon moving to

the UK, quickly observed the British habit of unnecessarily apologising.

> When you're in the supermarket, and there's a lot of people in the aisle, and you're all just doing your shopping, it's constant, 'Sorry, sorry, sorry', as you all reach for the items you want or try and get past each other with your trolleys. You don't need to say sorry. You're not being rude. You're all just doing your shopping. It's OK.

Cultural quirks and conditioning aside, this shows how quick we can be to apologise when we don't need to. What are you apologising for? *Existing?* By all means, be polite and say 'thank you' to someone who steps aside so you can get the peanut butter, but do you need to say 'sorry'? Probably not, unless you've run over their toes with your trolley. Consider this workplace example:

> Sorry to bother you. Could I talk to you about a little project idea I've had? Just when you've got a spare five minutes. I know you're busy, so I won't keep you.

It starts with an unnecessary apology. It's unnecessary because it's the workplace and the speaker is supposed to be interacting with others, not apologising for doing so. Then it dribbles away into self-diminishing waffle that undermines the benefit of the speaker's idea ('little'), puts all the power in the hands of the other person ('when you've got a spare five minutes'), and in stating the other's importance ('you're busy') undersells the importance of the speaker ('I won't keep you'). If you were the other person in this scenario, and a colleague said this to you, I doubt you'd feel compelled to listen to what they had to say. On the other hand, consider this second example:

> Good morning, I've had a project idea I'm really excited about. When are you free to discuss it?

That's so much better. It's still polite, but it's positive and far more likely to get the other person interested in what the speaker has to say. As part of your momentum mindset transition from a state of inertia, to achieving an incredible life, there will be times when you'll talk about yourself. That might be explaining lifestyle changes to family members, or speaking to potential customers about a new business. Please, don't apologise unless you've actually done something wrong. Sell your dream (to yourself and others) with positivity and a 'this is what I'm doing' attitude. Don't apologise and don't ask for permission. You have just as much right to improve your life, offer an idea, or launch a business as anyone else.

CHAPTER FIVE

The world around you

Don't waste your time chasing butterflies. Mend your
own garden and the butterflies will come.

> – Mario Quintana, poet

Look around

To get this far, you've done a lot of work on yourself. Looking
deep within and assessing the effect you can have on your future.
In many respects, that's the hardest part of this process. Getting
your internal world in order is no guarantee of success, however,
as you are always going to have to function within an external
world that you have relatively little control over. Events will
occur that you have no influence over. They may derail your
projects, or provide an unexpected boost. Though you may not
be able to influence them, you do have some ability to decide
how you react to them.

In this section of the book, we'll look at the external world and the factors which may stop you from reaching escape velocity, plus those that could help. The twenty-first century world of business is one of interconnectivity. Events that happen far away from you, or in an industry that appears to have nothing to do with yours, can have unexpected consequences on what you are trying to achieve. All it takes is one container ship to get stuck in a canal and businesses across the world suffer disruptions to their supply chains and cash flow. An unhelpful policy decision by a politician might result in a sharp increase in taxes or a decrease in available labour. Or a global pandemic closes the doors on your restaurant for months.

Unintended consequences and unforeseen events have just as much potential to wreak havoc on your personal life. You miss a flight because your car breaks down and you miss your sister's wedding. The kids leave a tap running overnight and you need to spend thousands on house repairs. A doctor's appointment confirms the worst and you have to drop everything to become a palliative carer.

Sorry, we know this is heavy. It's not pessimistic though. It's realistic because these are all possibilities. Life can be tough. We encourage you to think positively and optimistically, to dream big, but we also urge you to do so with your eyes open and to be prepared for things not going to plan.

Look around you, work out what you can influence, and think about how you can respond to the things you don't have control over. This will help give you clarity, give you comfort, and also avoid unnecessary stress.

Catalysts

Let's jump back into the science lessons, building on our knowledge of activation energy.

The scientifically-minded among you will know the activation energy required to start a reaction can be altered. It's not necessarily a fixed quantity. It can be modified with the use of a catalyst. Again, this is a simplified explanation, but a catalyst modifies the transition stage to lower the activation energy required by adding its own energy to the reaction.

Who, or what, are the catalysts who can help you? What catalysts can you use to lower the activation energy required from yourself? Your catalysts could be:

- A bookkeeper who will keep on top of your accounts so you can focus your attention elsewhere.
- A tutor to help you learn a new skill.
- Family members who look after your children while you attend a training course.
- Your massive bodybuilding neighbour who'll help get your broken down car rolling.

Think about everything you will need to do to reach your goal and identify all the areas where you can add in a catalyst to help lower the activation energy required from you.

Bear in mind that just because you are working hard doesn't necessarily mean you are applying that energy effectively. Applying that effort in the wrong direction, or in the wrong conditions could mean that energy is wasted. Every workplace seems to have that person who works late or makes a lot of noise about being busy, yet performs poorly. Don't be that person, the 'busy fool.'

Returning to the broken down car, it's going to be practically impossible to push it uphill, into a headwind, on a muddy, bumpy track; even with your massive bodybuilding neighbour lending you a hand. On a smooth road, with a gentle downhill gradient, and a following breeze, it will be far, far easier to move your car and build the required momentum.

This is why it's so important to create or find the optimum conditions to achieve your goal. What this means for you will depend on those goals and your personal circumstances. If you're writing a book, optimising your conditions might be as straightforward as finding a comfortable place to work and minimising distractions. If you're trying to launch a new product, there are more conditions to consider, from the micro (how you organise your desk) right up to the macro (the state of the global economy).

Some of these conditions you'll be able to change quickly and easily. Others will be more complicated and you may have little influence over them. This might mean waiting, but don't let that be an excuse for inaction. The *perfect* conditions might never come along, so you could be waiting forever. Instead, do what you can to make the conditions *better*. As we've already said, 'good enough is good enough.'

A steam powered rocket made of lead is never going to get off the ground. Build the lightest, strongest rocket you can, load it up with the right fuel, add a catalyst, point it in the right direction, light the ignition and soar.

Who we hang out with, we become

We are social animals. We crave freedom, but also need to belong. There are very few exceptions, who choose to live entirely separate from the rest of society. The vast majority of us - even if we think of ourselves as loners, or comfortable with just our own selves for company - require some human interaction.

'Belonging' is a safety net. It gives us the reassurance to try new things, and venture far away from the pack, with the reassuring knowledge that we have somewhere to return to. Our tribe will have our back if things go wrong. It's why we seek out collective experiences: mass-participation runs, supporting a football team, joining a book club, dancing in a mass of sweaty bodies, or attending a church.

There is power in the group. When you're head down, working on your plan to achieve an incredible life, remember to look up, re-engage with your fellow humans, and tap into that power. If the people around you are people you admire, who love you, or who support you, then the power will be even stronger.

> You will do better if you create intentional and purposeful relationships, based on mutual respect and growth.
> – Usha Raman, Founder of Nexus Training Group
> (Perth, Western Australia)

Don't be a stranger. You've got to get out there. Join groups. Pick up the phone to someone you know and say, 'Can I buy you a coffee?' You'll be amazed at the number of people who say, 'I'd love to.' It's incredible, the number of people who are in business and want to help others either get into business or do well.

- Paul Edwards, Director at Edwards Commercial Cleaning (Newcastle upon Tyne, UK)

Who travels with you?

Hopefully by now you know who you want (and who you don't want) travelling with you on your rocket towards an incredible life. This is great if you have ready access to the people who'll help you. If you're striking out on your own, in a new country, or with a new venture, for example, some community cultivation will be required.

Fortunately, like-minded people tend to be attracted to each other. To attract others into your orbit, you'll have to take on the values and actions that you seek in others. For example, if you need a mentor, but can't find one, offer yourself as a mentor to people who are at an even earlier stage of their careers. You may find you become part of a mentoring network and get to know someone who can be the mentor you need.

When you find that person, don't just assume they'll be able to read your mind and know that you need them. If you appear to be doing a grand job without them, they might just swing by your orbit and fly off into space again. Be vulnerable and ask for help when you need it.

I had to create a professional network because my business involves connecting industry with education and young people. I had only been in Australia for 18 months and didn't know anyone in business, so I had to create a whole professional network from nothing.
– Karen Dennett, Founder of Engaging Education (Perth, Western Australia)

Your inner circle

Think of five people who can help you reach escape velocity. Whether they offer practical business support or they're a shoulder to cry on, think about who helps you get the best out of yourself. Who always makes you feel energised and positive when you meet them? This top five is your inner circle. As there's five of them, we could use the analogy of a five-pointed star, with you in the middle, but that seems a bit spiky and uncomfortable. Also, don't worry too much about the precise number. It's not essential that it's exactly five, just as long as there are enough of them to offer you a wealth of support options, but not so many that it's hard to maintain meaningful relationships with them.

Over time, we become more like the people we spend the most time with, so choose your inner circle wisely. Surround yourself with the right people. For example, choose positive people who are driven, focussed and successful, and you may develop those traits too. For example, your inner circle could consist of:

- Amelia, your romantic partner.
- Brian, your business mentor.
- Charlie, your accountability buddy.
- David, your spiritual guru.
- Ella, your go-to friend for when you need to have some fun.

Of course, this group could change. There are various domains of wellness, and you may need different types of support at different times in your life. These could be emotional, physical, occupational, intellectual, financial, social, environment, or spiritual support. The example above includes a mix of the practical and romantic, the serious and the fun. In this way, most of the support areas are covered. Bear in mind, there's little value in having an amazing support network if you don't reach out when you need to. There is great strength in being vulnerable and asking for help.

To close this section, we'll also add that it might also be a little awkward to say, 'David, you have been selected to serve in my Inner Circle.' These aren't intended as official, titled positions with a badge or certificate (unless you decide otherwise!). It's an exercise to encourage you to think about who is important to you, and why. The flip side is that in doing so, you may identify people who you can support and recommit to doing so.

Optimism breeds optimism. If you're feeling a bit down, or not sure if you're going in the right direction, go hang out with some really happy entrepreneurs that are oozing with optimism because it is infectious. Be around people that light your spark, make you smile and make you laugh. I love being around people that are excited about the future and that inspires me. Then, I go into the studio and my optimism inspires the kids in turn.

– Carrie Anne Forsyth, Director at Esteem Dance Company (Perth, Western Australia)

It is lonely, and there isn't always anybody out there to help you. Actually, a lot of people aren't that supportive, especially if you're starting off on a new career track that's very different to what you did before. So I decided to buy a dog.

I'd always loved dogs and had one when I was in my teens. I bought a fox terrier, which ended up being two fox terriers, and they were with me all the way from 1993 to 2005. They were my companions and got me out of bed in the morning.

– Will King, Founder of King of Shaves (London, UK)

Interfaces

Years ago, Jonathan's father, Simon, told him, 'Everything is about interfaces.' They are where the potential for problems exist, but they are a fundamental part of any structure or relationship. Simon is an architect, so this concept is best illustrated with a construction analogy.

When building a house there are many potential problems, which almost always come down to the interfaces between different elements and materials. A failure to consider the interfaces can result in cracks, leaks and other issues.

A brick is a brick is a brick. On its own, it is a known constant. Place bricks together and you can build a wall. Without cement it may stand up, but could fail. Using cement adds a layer of complexity and means the job will take longer, but reduces the chance of failure. Get the brick-cement-brick interface wrong (too much, too little, not straight enough, etc.) and you will build a weakness into the structure that could cause problems at a later date.

Looking at the rest of the building, the individual elements may be sound, but it is the interfaces where problems can lie. Water, especially, will find and exploit a gap. The walls and roof may be watertight, but if the interface between the two is flawed, then the whole structure is flawed. The same is true of people at the interpersonal level.

- Different expectations.
- Different beliefs and values.
- Different cultures or languages.

- Different directions.
- Different moods.

The key is communication. It always is, as that is our primary human-to-human interface.

It's no secret that the best drama or sitcoms hinge on poor communication, as that is what creates dramatic tension. All drama contains conflict. That doesn't have to be violent conflict, but the sense of people or circumstances not being in alignment. The easiest way to achieve that is for two parties to be ignorant of the other's intent or actions because they haven't talked openly. Think about Ross and Rachel (in Friends), Niles and Daphne (in Frasier) and Romeo and Juliet (in Romeo and Juliet). Every television soap argument, ever, seems to result from a lack of effective communication. But in real-life, we're better off without that drama and can avoid it easily.

Clear, open communication keeps the interpersonal interfaces neat, tidy and watertight. No upsetting 'We were on a break' arguments. No years wasted watching the one you love marry another man. No accidentally both dying because one of you failed to mention the poison was a ruse. Just say how you feel, explain what you need, and ask what you can do to help the other person. It's as simple as that.

Everyone is wearing a mask

As well as self-compassion, show compassion to your fellow

humans. We're all dealing with sh*t of some description and, as Jonathan's former English teacher was fond of (perhaps inappropriately) telling him and his fourteen year old classmates, 'Sh*t rolls.' In that instance, the teacher was making the point that the school was assessed according to certain criteria, which meant the teachers had targets, which meant the pupils had work to do. That is often true within the vertical hierarchy of a school. It also applies, with a little variation, in more horizontal hierarchies such as social settings or the workplace. Except rather than roll down, it rolls sideways.[16]

For example: someone will have a problem that is stressing them out or getting them down. As much as they might think they're hiding it, some of it will leak out into their interactions with other people and cause them to be grumpy, angry, or just a bit rubbish at their job that day. In this way, it causes problems for the other people around them. You might be on the receiving end of this, or you might be the person causing the problems. You could even end up in a chain where someone's problems cause you problems, which you then pass on in turn.

Break the cycle with compassion. Recognise that most of us go around wearing a mask a lot of the time. We don't always know what is really going on as people tend not to air their dirty linen in public. Be mindful of the effect you have on others, and remember that someone causing you problems might be going through much worse themselves.

---

[16] There's a chance it'll roll through some glitter, and be presented to you by someone with a smiling face, but it's still a sh*t.

Vicki and Jonathan's razor

Hanlon's razor, attributed to computer programmer Roger J. Hanlon, states:

> Never attribute to malice that which is adequately explained by stupidity.

It's a fun philosophical approach, which can be useful to defuse problematic situations, but we prefer to approach life with a little more compassion, so we've edited it to provide a rule of thumb to follow when on your path to escape velocity:

> Never attribute to malice that which is adequately explained by an innocent mistake, or someone dealing with their own sh*t.

We like to work from the base assumption that people generally aren't out to get you, or to make your life difficult. If they happen to cause you problems, it's much more positive to assume that they did so either through an error on their part, or because they have something going on in their own lives that has caused them to behave in a way you perceive to be as bad.

Please, cut your fellow humans some slack. Offer them help if you think they need it. And if they persist in making life difficult for you, then you can take a harder stance if you want.

Balancing soft and hard skills

There's a lot of talk about critical thinking being limited by echo chambers. If we get our news from one source, only connect online with people who share our opinions, and move within one homogenous group of friends, then we only hear the voices that sound like our own. Our world view narrows, we miss out on the good stuff we don't know about, and we limit our ability to understand people who may be experiencing life in a different way to us.

The same is true of the workplace, where echo chambers of skills and experience can exist alongside echo chambers of ideas and opinions. This can lead to entrenched ideas that are never questioned, resulting in uninspired design, and a lack of growth or evolution.

It also builds in unnecessary risk. If everyone in a team has the same skill set, it is difficult to react effectively should an unexpected event occur that requires a different approach. A balanced team, with a wide range of skills, experiences and personalities will be better placed to adapt to whatever problems or opportunities come its way. Building a balanced team can be easier said than done, however.

If you were launching a business right now, and wanted help with your social media marketing, would you go for an expert in Facebook, TikTok or LinkedIn? Or would you go for the person who already has an eye on the next big thing and has proven they have the ability to adapt to new platforms?

Let's jump forward a few years. Your business is flying and you decide to take on a new manager to look after the production side of things. Who do you choose?

- The person with the best project management qualifications and years of experience at a top firm, but a reputation for being hard to please?
- Or the person with fewer qualifications and not as much experience, but who has demonstrated the ability to slot into new teams and get others to perform well without ruffling too many feathers?

It's a hypothetical scenario and reality is rarely so black and white, but these rhetorical questions do highlight the need to balance hard and soft skills in business (and our personal lives).

On the one hand, there will always be the hard, technical skills and expertise needed to perform the role, demonstrated by job-specific experience and qualifications.

On the other, there are the soft skills essential for a cohesive, well-performing team of people who thrive when they work together. Depending on the context, this may be communication, flexibility, creativity, leadership, and teamwork skills, for example.

Many of these soft skills exist on a spectrum. A great team worker who struggles to work solo would be at the opposite end of the scale to an amazing solo worker who struggles within a team. It might seem the ideal employee would sit at the halfway point, with all soft skill attributes set at 50%. There are two problems with this:

1. There probably isn't a 'perfect' average worker with

completely balanced soft skills, so you might never find them.

2. A team of people with identical characteristics is going to miss out on the wonderful creative spark and expanded range of thinking that comes from bringing different people together.

The first step to building a balanced team is to understand where you are currently. Map out the skills and experience already in your team and identify where the gaps are. It doesn't need to be a difficult task: a catch-up coffee chat with each of your colleagues can tell you what you need to know. This can guide future recruitment or help determine what training different team members should focus on.

Of course, a team made up of a range of very different individuals is going to require a range of different management styles and communication methods to get the best out of them. For example, Andy might require regular contact, but Bob does better with a bit more free rein. Understanding different personality types can be tricky, but there are tools to help, including the Entrepreneurial Mindset Profile®, which we discussed earlier.

The EMP was originally developed to help people identify how they compare to successful entrepreneurs and corporate senior managers, but is a valuable tool at all levels of an organisation. By answering the EMP questions, and interpreting them with the aid of a certified EMP practitioner, you can understand the different personality types within your team, how those personalities might interact with and complement each other, and where people can improve.

It's worth remembering that no matter how well you try and understand your team and recruit accordingly, it's unlikely you're ever going to have the perfect team consisting of people with optimised soft skills, i.e. the perfect balance of introvert and extrovert, thinker and doer, team player and solo performer.

That's OK, because as long as you understand the limitations of yourself and others, you can compensate accordingly. Embracing your positive traits and making them your unique selling point is how you can play to your strengths.

The above points are still valid considerations even if you're a sole trader doing your own thing, rather than trying to grow a large company. To support your work, there will always be people who become part of your team, even if just for a brief moment. You may use a website designer, a social media expert, an accountant, a mechanic to service your van, a printer, or a coach. On top of this are the friends and family members who form your emotional and personal support team outside of working hours.

For each of these relationships, the balance of hard and soft skills, plus personalities, will be just as important as if you were all in one office working together for the same organisation.

Your soft skills may transfer across to new opportunities, but if you're lacking the required hard skills, you may struggle to thrive. This is where it's so important to surround yourself with the right people.

This is a lesson Vicki was reminded of when preparing to launch the Get Unstuck Fast! Viscosity Podcast. She spent six hours editing the first episode before handing it over to a professional podcast editor who completed the job far quicker and to a much higher standard than Vicki could have done.

Not only that, the editor had so much valuable advice and insight, gained from years of working in the podcast world, that she would never have known about otherwise. If Vicki had persisted with doing it herself, she would have missed out on all this knowledge. The trick is to delegate to great people. Vicki also makes use of an accountant, bookkeeper, personal assistant, and graphic designer.

> There are three essential skills to have in business:
> 1.   Collaboration: build a network of people around you that you can learn from and share ideas with. There are a lot of challenges you can solve just because you have the right people around you.
> 2.   Delegation: especially when you're starting out, there are a lot of things to do and you should never try to do them all by yourself, otherwise you will end up wearing yourself down.
> 3.   Communication: effective communication can help when negotiating.
> > – Bukamu Dube, Director at Job Skills Training Academy (Perth, Western Australia)

A business such as ours (a dance school), would fall to pieces without succinct communication at all levels. Parents are busy juggling jobs and extracurricular activities, hence you need to have all channels of communication open to ensure every single person -

child, caregiver, grandma, as well as staff - know exactly what's going on and when. This is particularly the case with community events and concerts. Our communication channels need to be like a well-oiled machine in order for the business to run effectively. That communication starts with Brittany (my daughter and business partner) and I at the start of the week, having a quick meeting about the key things we need to communicate to staff and students.

Emotional intelligence is important to us because we have to be able to self-regulate. We have to be acutely aware of the way in which we relate to the children and families at all times. We're in the business of enhancing children's emotional intelligence as well because we, through dancing, are driving them to become intrinsically motivated learners, encouraging a team mentality and developing social skills.

– Carrie Anne Forsyth, Director at Esteem Dance Company (Perth, Western Australia)

Swerve the naysayers

Who do you *not* like spending time with? Be honest. Why do you not like spending time with them? Is it because of how they make you feel, or what they make you do? Are they a massive drain on your time, or leave you feeling emotionally drained?

Here's a potentially radical idea: could you cut them from

your life? We've already worked on your positive inner circle, so let's consider the opposite. Is there anyone specific - or types of people in general - who are going to be a hindrance in your journey from inertia to an incredible life? These could range from those who are so down all the time that they unintentionally kill the mood when they walk in the room, through to those who are actively working to prevent you from reaching your goals.

Write them down, then come up with a plan for each one. It's hard to avoid people entirely, so your plan should be a little more detailed than just 'ghost them until they go away.' After all, they may reappear when you least expect it, like characters in a horror movie. Instead, think of strategies for reducing their influence on you. How can you limit the time you spend with them? How can you respond when they say something negative? Or, do they have any good traits you can help them develop? Can you reorient your relationship with them so they become a positive influence rather than a negative one?

We'll let you determine the best response for the unhelpful or toxic people in your life, based on your circumstances and relationships. We will offer this note of encouragement, though: swerve the negative naysayers who will pull you down. Don't let people dull your sparkle. You are meant to shine.

> You've got to get rid of the naysayers in life. It's a difficult thing to do, as they could be family or friends. They're the people who *always* say 'I wouldn't do this,' or 'I wouldn't do that,' without offering positive

advice. You can't have that in your life.
- Paul Edwards, Director at Edwards Commercial
Cleaning (Newcastle upon Tyne, UK)

It is none of your business what anyone thinks of you. Everybody is judging everybody, but it doesn't matter as it doesn't make a difference. You can't control what people think, so don't worry about it.
– Jo Saunders, Founder of Wildfire Social Marketing
(Perth, Western Australia)

The stories we tell ourselves about others

Earlier in this book, we asked you to consider the stories about yourself that you have internalised. Those that come from within, or that others have given you. Now, we are asking you to recognise that you may also have internalised false stories about others, too. There's a chance that the people in your life may not be exactly as you've imagined them to be. They could be better than you've given them credit. Or they could be worse for you than you dare admit to yourself.

When thinking about the people in your life, do you ever find yourself thinking things such as 'They're not really a bad guy,' 'I can fix them,' 'It's just how they are,' 'I've never liked them,' 'They're just never going to change,' or so on?

Pause and be honest: are these thoughts true? Are you being too generous to them, or not generous enough?

Whichever way around it is, what does that say about you? It might well be the case that the people in your life don't need to change, but you need to change how you think about them. Perhaps the problem with the relationship is not how they behave, but how you interpret those behaviours and react to them.

Toxic or abusive relationships

We've talked about minimising your exposure to people who bring you down. Most of the time these people will be an irritant or distraction. They're unhelpful, but not dangerous, and you can usually find ways of avoiding them. Separate to this is another type of person; the abuser.

It is a lot harder to break free of the influence of someone who is abusing you, because they will actively do whatever they can to stop you from doing so. We're sorry if this section brings up unpleasant memories for you, but it is important to mention as it may help someone in danger.

The first step is to recognise if you are in an abusive relationship. There are different kinds of domestic abuse and some are easier to spot than others. All share the same characteristics of a forced imbalance of power.

- **Physical**: causing a bodily injury, either using weapons or the perpetrator's physical size and strength to overpower the victim.

- **Emotional**: using insults and criticism to destroy an individual's self-worth or state-of-mind.
- **Sexual**: involving sexual assault or rape. Also includes sexual humiliation and degradation, secretly filming or taking pictures, showing private pictures to others, deliberate infection with an STD, or coercion into having an unwanted abortion or pregnancy.
- **Tech**: keeping control over the victim's personal devices and online accounts, or using technology such as spy-ware to track their movements.
- **Psychological**: humiliating or embarrassing someone to control their behaviour.
- **Financial abuse**: this is the most common form and involves the abuser denying the victim access to money, controlling all their finances, or restricting their ability to earn their own income.

If any of the above are familiar to your personal situation, or that of someone you know, please get help. If you're unsure, but something doesn't feel right, go with your gut. Abusive behaviour is never acceptable. It's not your fault if you are a victim of domestic abuse, and there is no shame in asking for help. Depending on where you live, there will be different services available to you. Put your internet browser into 'incognito' or 'private browsing' mode, find those local to you, and reach out for help and support.

> The scariest thing I've done was walking out of a very toxic marriage with just my clothes, my shoes and a

box of books. It was scary and liberating and exciting and thrilling all at once. And I did it. I could have moved back to Singapore, but I decided I was going to stay in Australia in this amazing place that I love. I think I'm doing so much better for it.

– Usha Raman, Founder of Nexus Training Group
(Perth, Western Australia)

Boundaries

Imagine you've got a new puppy.[17] You're trying to set the ground rules. Don't sit on the sofa, don't pull the lead, this is where to eat, this is where to poo, etc. Consistent application of clear boundaries will help the puppy understand what is expected of them. This good behaviour training could all be undone if a friend looks after the puppy and has a completely different set of rules. To prevent this, you'll have to clearly explain the rules that you've set. Do this, and you, the puppy and your friend all get along. Don't do it, and chaos could ensue, with all your good work undone in one afternoon.

There's a balance to be found when it comes to having boundaries. On the one hand, it's beneficial to have clearly defined limits to what you are willing or unwilling to do or accept. On the other hand, if those boundaries are too solid, they can become a wall between you and other people.

---

[17] Shout out to Vicki's new dog, Leo!

If you don't demonstrate where your boundaries are, others may take advantage of you. We reckon this is rarely from malice, but due to them misreading where your boundaries are. Thus, they could overstep them unwittingly, unaware that what they perceive as you having a willingness to do something is actually not the case. You might have only wanted to give an inch, but they thought you were offering a mile. This can lead to burnout in the workplace as you get more and more work dumped on you. Or it can cause stress in your personal life as you run around trying to sort out everyone else's lives and neglecting your own wellbeing.

If your boundaries are too firm, however, others may perceive you as stubborn, unwilling to compromise, awkward to deal with, or antisocial. The key, as with so much in life, is communication. Don't be afraid to explain where your boundaries are. Doing so could feel uncomfortable, especially if you're not used to making your wishes clear. If you're not in the habit of putting yourself first, verbally setting out your boundaries to another person may not come naturally. Don't worry. Be reassured that by being clear up front, you're taking away the stress that arises from later uncertainty. So many conflicts or misunderstandings arise simply because the opposing parties haven't explained themselves properly. If expectations are set at step one, then the subsequent steps will be smoother.

To use a low-key example, imagine a colleague asking you to do some work for them. You've already got a lot on your plate, and could do without adding more work to your to-do list, but still reply 'Sure thing. I'll get it to you ASAP.' But because you're so busy, it will take you a few days to get to it. During that time, you'll get stressed because the task is glaring at you from your to-do list, and they'll get anxious or annoyed wondering when you'll get back to them. This could be avoided by setting a boundary at the beginning: 'Sure thing. I've got some other projects to work through, but I can get it to you on Wednesday.' Your colleague can relax because they know when they're getting the work from you, and you can relax as you're not going to have to deal with impatient chasing emails. It's not a selfish act, but a helpful one.

Other examples of boundary setting can range from 'I don't eat fish' (so your date knows not to book a table at a seafood restaurant), to 'I always take Friday afternoons off' (so you can attend a yoga class), to 'Be home by ten' (so your kids know where the line is). Humans are at their happiest when they know the boundaries of acceptable behaviour, but have freedom to operate as they wish within those boundaries. By defining your boundaries, you make it easier for other people to be happy when interacting with you.

You'll also be making yourself happier by exercising self-control and self-empowerment over your life. This will build your self-esteem and independence. Boundaries are healthy rules that - if both parties are clear on them - provide a map to help you navigate the relationships in your personal and professional life. With boundaries in place, you can grow within a safe environment, without being tired by the mental stress of uncertainty. The extra energy from reducing this stress will help you achieve your goals.

If boundary setting doesn't come naturally to you, you

may need to practise. Think of the situations in which you have found yourself doing things you didn't want to do, or not in the manner you would have liked. Was there an opportunity, most likely at the beginning of any interactions, where you could have set clear boundaries? What if you'd said 'No' instead of 'Yes' (or vice versa)? We don't want you to ruminate on past events excessively, as you can't undo the past, but recognising where and how boundaries were crossed can help you be prepared to prevent it happening in the future.

These don't have to be big, traumatic events. They could be the micro-irritants that litter our lives and can accumulate into an overall sense of being p*ssed off with everything: having to give the kids a lift, colleagues emailing you at the weekend, clients not paying you on time. If similar annoying events keep happening to you, is that because you've not been unclear about your boundaries and not stated that they're unacceptable?

If you're struggling to justify the setting of boundaries to yourself, let alone anyone else, draw a little picture of yourself in the middle of a page in your notebook. Draw a big circle around the picture of yourself. Within the circle, write down all the things you want to protect: things you want to do, time you want to spend with yourself, how you'd like other people to interact with you, and so on. The big circular line around you is the boundary that keeps those protected items close to you. Of course, you're not going to cover every eventuality or likely interaction with this exercise, but it can help to have a visual reminder of what your boundaries are for. They're to look after the parts of your life that you value. Therefore, it's important that you get comfortable with stating where those boundaries are. We can't assume that other people will instinctively know how we want to be treated. Take the lead and constructively teach people how to treat you.

The boundaries that are right for you *now*, may not be right for you in the future, so remain open to the possibility of change. If your boundaries are a bit squishy, or bendy, then you stand a better chance of being able to work in cooperation with people who have different ways of working to you. If your boundaries are slightly porous, like the cells on a leaf's surface which allow respiration to occur, then unexpected, potentially nourishing opportunities can find their way in.

As we're all aware, humans don't live in isolation, so a degree of compromise may be necessary. Your boundaries may be incompatible with those of others. Clear communication will stop this becoming a problem. Set out the reasons for your boundaries, and listen to them as they do the same. If you're both willing to bend a little bit, you'll soon find a middle ground that you both find acceptable, while also appreciating the effort each has made to accommodate the needs of the other.

If, after all this work on yourself, you're still saying 'Yes' to things you instinctively want to say 'No' to, ask yourself why that's happening. Is your head or your gut making the decision, and which is right? Is it because you're scared of losing work? Do you constantly feel the need to please everyone? Are you lacking in the confidence required to assert yourself? Are you wary of conflict? Do you just want to be liked? These are all bigger issues that you might have to do some extra work on, but recognising and addressing them is important. It will help break the cycle of poor boundary setting and help you protect those boundaries when you do set them.

Practice framing your boundaries on positive, rather than negative terms. 'Don't do X' becomes 'Please do Y.' People are far more likely to respond to positive instructions. If you then add an explanation, so the other person understands why you're asking them to do something in a certain way, then you'll have an even higher chance of them following your instructions. 'Please do Y because it helps me do Z.'

> I was raised by two very strong women. My mum was a solo parent, so her and my grandma raised me in a small town in Scotland. So that strong mindset is hard-wired in. When I've been faced with gender inequality (such as when I returned to work after my son was born), I will say, straight away, 'I'm not going to tolerate this' and nip any problems in the bud.
> - Karen Underhill, Founder of Blue Meanies Arts and Events (Newcastle upon Tyne, UK)

Prepare your No script

If you still find yourself saying Yes when you want to say No, prepare a 'No script'. We see this with friends and family members who, when faced with something they don't want to do, get anxious and come up with convoluted stories about why they're having to pull out. 'Thanks for the invitation, but I can't come to dinner with you this evening as Sandra's cat has chicken pox and is scratching itself raw. Her car has broken down, so I've got to go to the vet to pick up the ointment. I'd much rather have come out with you, but Sandra's going through such a tough time at the moment that I think it's best I stay here.' This is all instead of saying the truth, which is that you're knackered from working late all week. 'Thanks for the invitation, but I've been working late all week and I'm knackered, so I'll give it a miss.'

An invitation is not a demand, it's an offer you can decline. Yes, there are some social niceties to observe, and you might have to go to the occasional dinner date you'd rather avoid just to be polite, but you can say No. If you find it hard to do, practise it.

- 'Thanks for the job offer. I'm going to say No, because I'm fully committed until April and I don't want to do a bad job for you.'
- 'No, you'll just have to get a taxi, as I need the car to get to the gym.'
- 'No, he's not allowed on the sofa.'
- 'I'll look at this on Monday as the weekends are when I spend time with my partner.'

Think of possible scenarios, devise a response, and practice saying it, out loud, in front of the mirror. Keep going until it no longer feels awkward.

If you're still struggling to justify this to yourself, remember this point: when you say No, you're making space in your day to say Yes to other things. Being selective about what you commit to, helps you to be more helpful to others, or more efficient and productive at work.

> I think it is very important to say 'No'. Sometimes saying No is actually good for the person asking you. Because if you take on another thing, then another thing, then you can spread yourself too thinly and not be of any help to them at all.
> – Dr Christopher Kueh, Design Abilities Specialist
> (Perth, Western Australia)

Setting boundaries with technology

The always-on nature of modern communication methods can make it fiendishly difficult to set boundaries and stick to them. Not only do mobile phones make it easier for other people to get in touch with us, but the devices are so addictive we can end up breaking our own screen time rules without realising we're doing it.

To help you set boundaries, get familiar with the settings on your phone:

- Make use of the 'Do Not Disturb' setting.
- Mute all group chats.[18]
- Turn off all but the essential notifications.

---

[18] It is rare for group chats to contain time-sensitive messages. If someone wants something urgently, they'll send you a message directly.

- Put your working hours into your email signature.
- Don't even look at your phone until you've carried out whatever personal morning routine you've chosen for yourself.

These are just five easy steps that will help you reclaim a little time for yourself each day. If you think you need stronger technology boundaries, Jonathan's approach may be helpful. Jonathan will readily admit to being easily distracted. Put some words in front of him - a book, magazine, leaflet, article, whatever - and he'll find himself reading them, rather than doing what he was supposed to be doing. Because he's aware of it, he puts systems in place to avoid such distractions. Thanks to the ready availability of things to read on smartphones, he is strict with his use of technology.

- When he's at home, Jonathan turns his phone off between 9pm and 8am, and avoids taking it into the bedroom.
- He uses the Minimalist Phone app to make his phone less visually distracting.[19]
- He makes sure it is hidden from view or out of his eyeline (especially when working, spending time with people, or having a conversation).
- He has no personal social media accounts because he found them too distracting (and because they were

---

[19] At the time of writing, only available for Android phones.

neither beautiful nor useful[20]).

This isn't about being a luddite, or deliberately awkward. Technology can be great, and no doubt there are plenty of people who have perfectly healthy relationships with their phones. But for Jonathan, these are the personal decisions he has made to make sure that he is in control of his technology, rather than the other way round.

Expectation setting

If you don't set clear expectations this can often lead to disappointment and regret. When we don't clearly define our expectations or communicate them to others, we open the door for misunderstandings, assumptions, and unmet needs. Again, this is all about communication and interfaces. Set boundaries, explain your intentions, and make your expectations clear. When it comes to expectations, anything less than total clarity leaves the window open for misunderstanding to creep in and cause problems.

    If you don't clearly communicate your expectations to a friend or partner, they may not understand what you need from them in a particular situation. They may make assumptions about what you want or need, which may not align with your actual expectations. This can lead to frustration,

---

[20] To paraphrase the nineteenth century poet and designer, William Morris, who we'll mention again.

disappointment, and even conflict if your needs are not met.

Similarly, if we don't set clear expectations for ourselves, we may struggle to achieve our goals or feel a sense of disappointment or regret. If you have a vague goal of 'getting in shape,' but don't define what that means or set specific steps to achieve it, you may not make progress or feel satisfied with your efforts.

Setting clear expectations is essential for creating a sense of clarity, purpose, and direction in our lives. When we clearly define our expectations, we are more likely to achieve our goals, build stronger relationships, and avoid unnecessary regrets and disappointments.

Don't under-sell yourself

If someone is asking you to do something, it's probably because they cannot, or do not want to do it themselves. Your value correlates not just to your ability to do it for them, but the potential *upside* to them of you doing so.

If you're setting a price, don't just base it on the time it'll take you, but on the benefit to them. If you stand still for an hour and it earns someone else a million dollars, then you deserve a big chunk of that cash, no matter how little effort it requires from you.

It's worth remembering that this applies to non-paid, non-business interactions too. A small act from you can have a massive effect on someone else. A thank you note might take you five minutes, but improve someone's whole day. Use this power wisely. A small act of love can make a whole world of difference to someone who is struggling.

Contribution

Never, ever forget that we're social animals that thrive in a community. Even if you spend time away from the tribe, on your journey of self-discovery, come back from time to time to share your findings with others.

'Self-help' can be seen as selfish. Enriching yourself (spiritually, emotionally, or financially), but ignoring everyone else. That's not living an incredible life. It may feel good for a while, but sooner or later that one-sidedness will gnaw away at the foundations inside your soul and bring you down.

Vicki loves philanthropy and being of service to others. Six years ago, she spent a couple of months supporting a project to raise money for a school in South Africa. The school sent a video of all the kids dancing and singing outside on a beautiful summer's day. The kids were shouting, 'Thank you, Auntie Vicki.' By coincidence, the video came through on the day Vicki ended a relationship. It was a bittersweet day, but one that filled her heart with the joy of giving back.

If you've got what you need, give back to others. Share the wealth, wisdom and love.

Team dynamics

For those who don't follow sport, you may not be aware that Sarina Wiegman was the coach who took the England women's football[21] team to victory in the 2022 European Championships. It may have been the first major tournament victory by an English national football team in 56 years, but it's not Wiegman's. In 2017 she won the Euros with the Netherlands and almost won the World Cup with them two years later. Simply put, she's a winner.

Television and newspaper interviews given by the England players during the tournament gave a glimpse into what makes Sarina's side so special, and what we - in business, sport and our personal lives - can learn from the Wiegman Way. Ultimately, it comes down to the interlinking concepts of Communication and Trust.

These are concepts we've already touched upon, so this shouldn't come as a surprise, but does show that if you get the fundamentals right, magic can happen.

When you're bringing together 23 elite sportspeople - all playing for different clubs, with different personalities, and different ambitions - and moulding them into a unified team, communication is vital.

It appears this process of clear communication started early on, as Wiegman said, 'We agreed on a couple of things about behaviour and they weren't just words, we lived it.' Note the word 'We'. This isn't Wiegman laying down the law and

---

[21] Or 'soccer', if you'd rather.

saying, 'I told them how to behave and they did it'. It's a collaborative, open approach. A conversation, not a command. Naturally, there are roles and hierarchies, but explaining this from the outset results in a shared culture designed with and for the people within it.

Wiegman's use of a fixed starting eleven and substitutes who can make an impact was a talking point. If her tactics had been poorly explained to the team, then it would be easy for players to become competitive with each other, or disappointed they've not been given the role they expected.

Using the forwards as an example, Ellen White was one of the most experienced players in the team. She was a key player at Manchester City with over 100 caps for the national team. Alessia Russo, ten years White's junior, was a rising star at Manchester United, and Nikita Parris was a Champions League winner who had been playing at the top level since she was a teenager. Without clear communication, they might view each other as rivals, which could have led to disharmony within the team.

Instead, White knew her role was to use her ability and experience to establish control of the game early on, and wear out the opposition goalkeeper and defence. This set the stage for Russo to come on and kill the game off with fresh legs and audaciously creative goals such as the back-heeled nutmeg against Sweden.

While White and Russo got most of the attention, Parris also played an important role. Coming on as an injury-time substitute in the knock-out stages, Parris only played a few minutes of the tournament. But those were crucial minutes in which it was important to have a cool head on the pitch. Rather than winning the game, her role was helping to ensure England didn't lose.

Each players' role will have been devised by Wiegman and her coaching team, based on a thorough understanding of the skills of each player and how they fit together. They will have then been explained clearly to each player. Even those who didn't play a single minute on the pitch will have known the importance of their roles as emergency substitutes or how they could help on the training ground.

This is supported by Keira Walsh, who said, 'Everybody knows where they stand so there's no guessing games behind closed doors and I think that does take the pressure off. The mentality now is just all about doing the best for the team and the team winning, rather than individuals. I think you can see that in the way we play.'

That clarity gave each player the freedom to perform at their best. Chloe Kelly said how she had the freedom to have fun and express herself. No doubt this freedom came with at least a few constraints and expectations, otherwise chaos and confusion could reign. But by defining the boundaries, Wiegman gave the players the freedom to do what they do best within those boundaries.

This display of trust from the manager ('I trust you to do your job') will breed trust from the players towards the manager ('I trust you to get the best out of me'), and towards each other ('I trust that you'll have my back').

How does this relate to business and entrepreneurship? There are three key points to observe:

1. Know your personality and skill-set, and that of your partners and colleagues. Are you the creative idea generator like Ella Toone, the cool headed leader like Leah Williamson, or the reassuring problem stopper like Mary Earps? What are you good at, and what do you need support with?

2. Communicate clearly. If you want someone to do something for you, they need to know exactly what it is you want them to do! Positivity can go a long way here, especially if you're dealing with a high-pressured situation, but don't shy away from honesty.

3. Create an environment of trust and freedom. A 2011 Gallup poll revealed the most engaged employees are those who have clearly defined roles and are then given the freedom to get on with their work in the way they consider best. There is a lot of room on the scale from complete autonomy to overbearing micromanagement, and the sweet-spot for each employee may be in a different place, but if you find it the whole team will perform perfectly.

These concepts are common sense. Putting them into practice, however, can be tricky when dealing with all the pressures of working life. If everyone is striving towards the same goal (literally in the case of a football match), this momentum can be enough to carry you through the difficult moments.

Love your team

If you're going into a new space, be aware there are unknown unknowns. Even if you think you are aware of all the possible problems and opportunities, there will almost certainly be things you hadn't considered or even realised were possible. The advice of an expert, who has experience of such matters, can save a lot of bother, stress and money and help you succeed.

Filling in the gaps in your own knowledge and skills can be achieved in a variety of ways. One of the most enjoyable ways to develop your knowledge is to expand the range of people and ideas you engage with, whether that's employees, colleagues, customers, books, or even just the podcasts you listen to.

Occasionally this may involve breaking out of your echo chamber. Very few people actively seek out opinions that challenge their world view, as doing so is uncomfortable. It's important though, as it leads to growth and improves your ability to handle the unexpected.

This is true even beyond the world of work. It is always important to surround yourself with the right people. Step one, if you want to build an effective team of experts, is to assess where your blindspots are. An EMP can help you achieve this.

Once you've gathered your experts, make use of your team, but don't exploit them. Recognise and celebrate their expertise. Take time to understand what makes them tick. Make them feel loved!

Coaches and mentors

Jonathan runs for fun, and to compete, albeit at a fairly modest level. Even though he's been running for years, and has built up a lot of knowledge on how to train, he has a coach he works with. Not only does Noel, the coach, have almost three decades more experience than Jonathan, but he helps prevent Jonathan from falling into bad habits or losing motivation or focus.

Given freedom to choose his own training, Jonathan would slip into prioritising the runs he most enjoys, which might not be the ones that will help him improve the most. Noel will set a training plan that balances the two.

They also have meetings a few times a year to review the training block they've just completed, and assess the progress against Jonathan's running goals. This is something Jonathan could do himself, but it's better when done with someone who offers another perspective.

If having a coach to help with a hobby can be useful, then having a life or business coach can be massively beneficial.

As well as a coach, a mentor is a good person to have by your side. They may seem similar, and there's overlap, but there's a difference. A coach may be more technical, or task specific, whereas a mentor is more likely to offer moral support or provide an example of good behaviour. A mentor doesn't even need to be working in the same sector as you, as their role is to act as an 'elder'; someone to look up to.

I didn't realise how important a coach or mentor was until I had one. When you're in your business, day in, day out, with no-one else to be accountable to, it can be difficult to stay focussed. You also forget how important it is to value yourself and celebrate your wins, instead of being hard on yourself when you have minor setbacks.

Having a business mentor has been invaluable for keeping me up to date with things like KPIs or future business planning. Vicki gave me so many tools and so much insight into work-life balance and how to celebrate the wins. It is inspiring and encouraging to have someone there to reinforce your strengths.

– Carrie Anne Forsyth, Director at Esteem Dance Company (Perth, Western Australia)

Accountability partners

Both coach and mentor can act as an accountability partner. This is what it sounds like: someone you are accountable to. In many workplaces, this will be your line manager. If you're your own boss, a freelancer, don't work in a vertical hierarchy structure, or want to be more accountable in your personal life, then your accountability partner could be anyone. A sibling, parent, colleague, or friend. It could even be a complete stranger. The idea is to periodically (daily, weekly, monthly, or whichever interval feels appropriate to you) tell that person what you intend to do. Then, at the end of that period, you tell them if you did it. It's as simple as that, but can keep you on track.

Detox and declutter your life

Multi-tasking is a myth.[22] The reality is that our brains switch rapidly from one task to another. It's like spinning plates: We have to jump from one, to the next, to another and so on, constantly switching our focus to keep all the plates from smashing on the ground. With a bit of practice, a couple of plates might be fairly easy. Keep adding in plates and at some point you're going to miss one and it will fall to the ground. This is what our brains are like with all the stuff we have to think about. There are two strategies for dealing with this:

1. Reduce the number of plates.
2. Get someone else to do the spinning for you.

The second option is appealing and you might be able to achieve it with delegation or sharing your concerns with others. However, its effectiveness will always be limited by the availability of suitable people to help you out. Therefore, reducing the number of plates is always going to be the best place to start. With this in mind, we urge you to detox and declutter the f*ck out of your life. What plates can you let drop without any problems? And which plates do you just want to throw out the window? Write down:

•   All the things that are currently annoying you.

---

[22] There has been a great deal of research on this subject. For a summary, read the article, 'Multitasking: Switching costs', on the American Psychological Association website. There's a link in the bibliography at the end of the book.

- All the admin things you need to do, but haven't.
- Loose ends you need to tie off.
- Conversations you need to have.

As always, be honest with yourself. Then keep going:

- What clothes can you get rid of?
- Is there too much visual clutter in your home or work environment?
- Are there financial outgoings you can reduce or get rid of?
- What eating habits aren't doing you any good?
- Are there substances in your life (e.g. alcohol, cigarettes, drugs) you might be better off without?

The fewer stressors you have in your life, the easier it will be for you to get stuff done with a clear, focussed mind. There's a balance of course. Super-minimalist environments work for some people, but we personally feel it is more beneficial to have some personal touches in your home. The nineteenth century designer and writer, William Morris had the right idea, when he said, 'Have nothing in your houses that you do not know to be beautiful or believe to be useful.'

We'd go further and say, 'Have nothing, *including people*, in your *life* that isn't beautiful or useful.' By all means, when you've already achieved your incredible life, and you have all the time, money and space in the world to accumulate stuff, go ahead and do so if that's what you want. But until then, while you're still stuck in your state of inertia, you've got to be making life as detoxified and decluttered as possible.

When Vicki moved back to the UK from Australia she got rid of six bin liners of clutter from her home office. She is now paperless and can work wherever there is space for a laptop. All her paperwork and admin is online. Jonathan likes to fill his working life with notebooks and books, but is able to hide them away at the end of the day to reduce how much mental space they occupy when he isn't working. Your job might require a certain amount of stuff. There's no getting rid of a massage therapist's need for a couch, a carpenter's tools, or an artist's materials, for example. However, we wouldn't mind betting there are some things you can do without. Holding onto stuff you don't need, or that doesn't improve your quality of life, will hold you back. It will hinder rather than help you. Get rid of it and move on. Build speed, maintain momentum, travel light.

Streamlining

If you're a helpful sort of person, you can rapidly find that your entire life is taken up looking after other people, and constantly putting yourself second. This is what happens when our actions occur passively, as a result of other people's expectations on us. To achieve an incredible life, get in the habit of acting intentionally: doing only what you have actively decided to do. That could still involve helping other people, should that be something you intentionally choose to do.

Declutter your to-do list or your regular obligations by

categorising everything that other people are expecting you to do. Go through all the jobs and commitments you apparently 'need' to do and work out whether that is truly the case. Which ones can you:

- Drop immediately?
- Drop soon, with a little bit of planning by you?
- Drop soon, with planning by someone else (i.e. give them notice)?
- Do less of, or do with readjusted boundaries?

Once you've done this, and have created some space for yourself, you can ask yourself a very important question: what do *you* want to do?

Things are easier with other people around you

There is a fascinating body of research that demonstrates the power of social support when approaching a difficult task. In one experiment, participants accompanied by a friend estimated a hill to be less steep when compared to participants who were alone. In another, participants who thought of someone they liked perceived a hill to be less steep than participants who thought of someone they felt neutral about, or disliked.[23]

[23] Simone Schnall, Kent D Harber, Jeanine K Stefanucci & Dennis R Proffitt, 'Social Support and the Perception of Geographical Slant', *Journal of Experimental Social Psychology*, Vol. 44, No. 5, 2008.

Another series of experiments asked participants to estimate the weight of a box before lifting it, and then reassess their estimate after lifting. Participants who performed the tasks on their own estimated the box to be heavier than those who performed the tasks with someone else.[24]

These, and other studies, prove the power of social support. Not only do tasks feel easier with others because of the practical assistance, but just knowing you'll have help makes a challenge seem less daunting. This is true both before the challenge and during it. The effect of social support on perception of effort is even more effective if the person working with you is someone you like.

This is why it is so important to surround yourself with the right people.

---

[24] Adam Doerrfeld, Natalie Sebanz & Maggie Shiffrar, 'Expecting to lift a box together makes the load look lighter', *Psychological Research*, Vol. 76, 2012.

CHAPTER SIX

Prepare your plan

The most difficult thing is to act, the rest is merely tenacity.

– Amelia Earhart, aviation pioneer

You can achieve an incredible life

By this point in the book, you'll have learnt about yourself and understand how to interact more productively with your inner and external world. The final step is to put it all into action.

You know what you want to break free from. You know the internal factors that have got you stuck in a state of inertia. You know the external factors in life and business that can impact you. You know what an incredible life looks like for you.

This part of the book will help you put everything you now know into practice, so you can get on with the wonderful work of building and maintaining momentum, reaching escape velocity, and achieving an incredible life.

Barbell strategy

To achieve your incredible life, you'll need to make a plan. For the best chance of success, ensure that your plan allows for the possibility of things happening that are out of the ordinary.

The essayist and former trader, Nassim Nicholas Taleb, describes how a 'barbell strategy' can balance risk and make the most of unexpected events by focussing on opposite ends of a scale. At its most simple, the strategy is this: if you were only to aim for the middle ground you may be unprepared should an extreme event happen. But if you were prepared for the extremes, you would thrive in unexpected scenarios.[25]

Bear this in mind when making your plans. Cover all bases. Do some scenario planning by letting your imagination run wild and writing down all the events - good or bad - that could affect your progress. Then, spend some time working out how you would respond. For example:

- Could you cope with being made redundant?
- What if you receive more orders than you can fulfil?
- What happens if you get hacked?
- Do less of, or do with readjusted boundaries?

These examples could be considered as problems, or they could be seen as opportunities. The difference is in how you react.

---

[25] Nassim Nicholas Taleb, *Antifragile*, Penguin, 2012.

Left or right?

In the UK, road running race routes tend to be anti-clockwise in direction. The opposite is true in Chile. This has absolutely nothing to do with the Earth's gravitational pull, or flushing toilets in different hemispheres. Instead, it is simply to minimise the number of roads that need to be closed to vehicle traffic.

In the UK, and the other 70+ countries where people drive on the left, a left-hand turn at a junction can almost always be completed without crossing any other traffic lanes. A right-hand turn will usually require movement across at least one lane, which adds an extra layer of risk and organisational complexity. Therefore, road running race routes in countries where people drive on the left tend to include more left-hand corners, meaning they are generally run in an anti-clockwise direction. The opposite is true in the 160+ countries where people drive on the right, such as Chile.

How is this relevant? Because it illustrates the point that best practice in one context could represent a terrible decision in another. If you're a British running race organiser using Chilean event management guidelines, without adapting them appropriately, you could find yourself causing traffic chaos, or getting people run over.

By all means, look to the market leaders, the experts in your field, or the people you trust, for guidance, but don't blindly accept their advice or follow their examples. Recognise that what worked for them might not work for you. The changes required may be simple - such as switching left-hand turns for right-hand turns - or they may require a little more thought. Either way, be careful to make sure that your plans are the right ones for you.

Fear of missing out

Know when to back off. You can't do everything, and nor should you. Focus on doing *something* and doing it as well as you can. Or, as well as you can on any given day.

Yes, you've got to be alert to new opportunities, but try to target the right ones. Don't let the fear of missing out (FOMO) force you to try and do everything. You'll either spread yourself too thinly and do a rubbish job, or burn out and do a rubbish job. Neither outcome is positive.

FOMO, in the personal or business world, can lead to anxiety and a lack of energy. You don't need that kind of stress in your life. Let it go. Be patient, be selective, be picky.

Timing

Person A: 'The key to good comed-'
Person B: 'IS TIMING!'

It's a classic joke, and a true one. As with comedy, the key to making positive life choices is timing. We want you to take action, but we also want you to take action at the right time.

Sometimes, that means waiting. You need to recognise when it's right to continue as you are. As desperate as you are to make a change, there may be benefits to staying put for a moment longer. Waiting may give you the time to resolve a tricky situation, get valuable work experience, or save the money you need for the next step.

It can be difficult to be sure exactly when the time is right. Make the most of the information you have available. If there isn't any, trust your gut and intuition. Then, when you think the timing is right, go for it.

Be seen

Unless your idea of an incredible life is to be a hermit, you're going to have to put yourself out into the world. At some point you'll need to sell something, whether that's a product you've made, a service you can offer, your skills and experience to an employer, or an idea to your colleagues. To do so, you'll need to be seen, even if just for an instant. To be seen, you'll need to stand out.

Depending on the context and what it is you want to achieve, that might be done in a low-key way (small-scale, one-to-one networking; sharing your work in specialist publications; or placing an ad in a local paper), or very 'noisily' (social media campaigns; speaking at conferences; or TV advertising).

However you choose to do it, it can be tough to get others

to notice you. This is especially true if you're trying to enter a saturated market. You can either directly compete against your competitors and try to do what they do, or highlight what makes you different and focus on that. We recommend the latter.

You know your superpower, as you identified it earlier. If you're selling a service you offer, where client relationships are important, focus on your superpower. People buy from people. Given the choice of two coffee shops, each with a comparable product, with similar décor, located next to each other, you're likely to opt for the one with the staff you like most, right?

If you're selling a product, what is that product's superpower or unique selling point? Is it cheaper, faster, stronger, more effective, or better looking than the competition? Find your point of difference, shout about it, and be seen.

> You don't need to reinvent the wheel, you just need to make the wheel a little bit different or a little bit better. We're not the first people who have ever developed a cleaning company. What we did though, is ask, 'How can we make it better for clients? How can we make the experience better?' Find your unique selling point.
> - Paul Edwards, Director at Edwards Commercial Cleaning (Newcastle upon Tyne, UK)

Simplify to amplify

When you're trying to be seen, keep your message clear. Deliver it cleanly. Make it easy for people to understand what it is you're saying. Don't overcomplicate things. Work out your key message and repeat it.

Once you've got their attention, then you can go into detail. Before that, when you're yet to catch their interest, simpler is better than louder. Simplify to amplify.

> If you're stuck in a rut, unhappy with what you're doing, and want to get to a better place - financially or just general life happiness - the first thing to do is think about what you're going to do.
>
> If you're going to compete against existing products or services, you've got to be very clear about what differentiates you from everyone else who will have been spending months and years thinking the same thing as you. Have a very clear *raison d'être* and a very clear mission statement with a singularity of purpose about what you do and why.
>
> – Will King, Founder of King of Shaves (London, UK)

You're doing OK

Happiness starts from within. We've asked you to do a lot of self-reflection and that isn't always easy. This is why self-compassion is so important.

When you're looking at mistakes you've made, don't be

too hard on yourself. Acknowledge any errors, look at what could be done differently next time, and move on. The present can be hard enough, without you adding in the troubles of the past, too. There's no 'Undo' or 'Delete' button in life, but you can choose what comes next. Mistakes can be the most valuable lessons. So choose to live authentically and be kind to yourself.

We're also asking you to put a lot of work in, but that's only because we want you to have the life you deserve. We recognise that the bigger the change, the harder it is for new actions to become habits. It takes time to reprogramme your old thought patterns, so there will be a period when it feels like you're constantly struggling against your existing mental muscle memory. Please be reassured that eventually those new changes will become second nature, and not feel so difficult.

Until that happens, there may be moments when you want to ease off on the constant self-improvement work and give yourself a break. That's absolutely fine. No-one can be 'perfect' all the time. We don't expect you to be, and neither should you. Perfection does not exist. Constant striving is exhausting if you don't remember to rest and take the pressure off. Sometimes, the best thing you can do is sit down and say to yourself, 'I'm doing OK.' Cut yourself some slack. Don't get hung up on everything you still need to do, but reflect on how far you've come. Be kind to yourself. When your energy and motivation returns, get back up and crack on again.

Do the things that scare you

The path to self-improvement is not always comfortable. Often, it is the opposite. To make progress, you're going to need to step into uncertain territory and do things that you'd really rather not do. Dale Carnegie, the writer and lecturer, wrote:

> Inaction breeds doubt and fear. Action breeds confidence and courage. If you want to conquer fear, do not sit home and think about it. Go out and get busy.

We'll acknowledge that if you're in a dark place, dealing with anxiety or fear, having someone say 'Stop worrying and just get on with it' might not be the most helpful or appropriate advice. Approached in the right way, however, Carnegie's words have an element of truth to them. You can't beat fear by ignoring it. Instead, get out in the world and do things, to help reset your state of mind. It might not be right for you, but it worked for us.

Caveat: the following is based on Jonathan's experience and may not be appropriate for you. We're <u>not</u> medical professionals. If you think you may have an anxiety disorder, or are living with depression or another mental health condition, we urge you to get professional help.

For pretty much the entirety of his twenties, Jonathan lived with what resembled an anxiety disorder. He can't say for certain whether it was, because he never got officially diagnosed or sought professional help. This is despite spending all that time knowing something was wrong and that he should probably do something about it. But he didn't, because he was too scared to do so, on account of the probable-anxiety disorder. Such is the difficult nature of such problems.

If he had to hazard a guess, he'd say it was likely he had some kind of social anxiety disorder and agoraphobia. It shape-shifted a little over that time, so it's tricky to pin down. More often than not, it presented itself in two ways: dread at the prospect of social interactions (more so with old friends and family members, than meeting new people); and a fear of any kind of situation in which he couldn't leave (waiting rooms and queues were particularly tough).

This led to irritable bowel syndrome which made certain situations even more panic-inducing (such as the period between entering the boarding gate and the seatbelt light coming off after take-off; or sitting in a theatre during a performance). These problems made life difficult. He missed out on social occasions, neglected friendships, and failed to enjoy holidays, weddings, or so many of the events that make life wonderful. Looking back, it wasn't a great time in many respects.

Now, at the age of 38 (at the time of writing), some of the symptoms persist, but they're far less significant than they used to be. Perhaps a 3/10 on a particularly bad day, rather than the constant 8+/10 they used to be.

This improvement hasn't just happened by itself, but is the result of a determined effort not to let anxiety (including anxiety about feeling anxious) rule his life. There wasn't a defined plan, as such, but a series of decisions that - at least in this unscientific study of one individual - seem to have helped.

These are:

- Confide in someone you trust.
- Address the cause of the feelings of social anxiety.
- Confront the situations that scare you.[26]

Taking each of these in turn, this is Jonathan's experience, described in his words:

Confide in someone you trust

> I am fortunate I have Heather in my life. We met when I was twenty, we moved in together at twenty-one, and got married at twenty-five. She met me at a time when my mental health difficulties were less pronounced, which meant she noticed when they got worse. When you're living with someone in a small flat (and you do almost everything together because you don't know anyone else in the city you've moved to) you tend to spot if they're having a bad day.
>
> Heather, out of concern for me, wouldn't let me hide my troubles from her and I am very grateful for that. Talking about the problems took the edge off them. It also meant that I had an ally in the room when we were out together. If I wasn't feeling great, I

---

[26] There's a possible fourth act, which may have been a coincidence, but does correlate with the IBS improving: become a vegetarian. Admittedly, correlation does not imply causation, so becoming a vegetarian may not solve all your problems, but Jonathan's going to stick with a meat-free diet, regardless.

could catch her eye and she would know what it meant. You have to be careful that the other person doesn't become a crutch – and that you become incapable of doing anything without them – but having someone else who knows how you're feeling is a massive help.

Address the causes

A lot of my anxiety about social situations was caused by the prospect of someone asking 'What do you do?' or 'How's work?'. At the time, I was 'under-employed' in a job I didn't enjoy. If anyone had thought 'That's a rubbish job' or 'Jonathan could do better than that,' they certainly didn't tell me. The anxiety was not caused by anyone else. It was internal, and related to my own feelings of inadequacy or underachievement.

There were, as I saw it, two options: change my relationship with the job; or change the job. Ultimately, I achieved the latter, but it was complicated and delayed by my not knowing what I wanted to do. The post-2008 economic downturn limited opportunities too, which didn't help. My values were leading me towards the arts and charities, but I had no relevant experience in either of those, which meant I couldn't get a paid job. To overcome this, I volunteered for different organisations in my spare time. It was a slog, doing voluntary work on top of my paid job, but had multiple benefits: I gained a greater understanding of the different roles that existed in these organisations; I got experience for my CV; and I was taking positive action that helped me rewrite the negative narrative I'd created about myself.

It took years, but once I got a foot in the door of the charity world, and was doing work I enjoyed, my social anxiety reduced. This increased my self-belief, I started seeking other opportunities, and the anxiety reduced yet further. I don't want to promote the idea that self-worth can only be derived from the work you do, as I think it is far more preferable to be happy regardless of your job title, but it would be disingenuous to claim that it wasn't significant for me.

Confront the situations that scare you

Again, Heather was a massive help as she encouraged me to do the things I was scared to do: travel, get a haircut, go to the dentist, go to the cinema, see friends and family, get on a rollercoaster, and other situations where I would worry that I couldn't leave, and thus feel trapped. Each time I did them, and nothing bad happened, it made it easier for me to do it the next time. It wasn't an instant cure, as my brain would find some new aspect to worry about: 'It was OK last time, but what if...?' The more I did, though, the better I felt. As reassuring as it was to have Heather's support, I also knew I needed to do things on my own.

I can't remember exactly when, as a lot of that

period is a stressed, anxious blur, but at some point I made the decision to deliberately seek uncomfortable situations and confront them head on. I organised a reunion of university friends, put together a networking group of fellow charity fundraisers, and donated blood. I started saying 'yes' rather than 'no'. I tried to spend more time doing things and less time worrying about them. I'm definitely not cured – I still feel nervous whenever I get a haircut, I'm in no hurry to get an MRI scan again, and the idea of a long-distance bus trip is terrifying – but I am so much better than I was.

A new friend recently told me he was surprised when I had told him I'd previously struggled with anxiety. Another said, 'I forget you have a job, as you always seem so relaxed.' To a degree, this is because I've learnt to mask my anxiety, but it's also because anxiety is now such a small part of my life, and I am so much more relaxed than I was. Undoubtedly, doing things I worry about has been a massive part of my recovery.

At first, Jonathan's approach had been accidental (he did things he didn't want to do, because he *had* to do them). Once he noticed improvements, it became more deliberate (he did things he didn't want to do, because he *chose* to do them).

After his (self-diagnosed) anxiety and agoraphobia improved, Jonathan spent time looking into his experience and realised his self-treatment resembled aspects of Exposure Therapy. This is often used as part of Cognitive Behavioural

Therapy. It involves the patient confronting the thing that scares them, without 'escaping' from it (i.e. by leaving the room, or performing compulsive acts). In time, this progressive exposure desensitises the patient. The fear response to the trigger stimuli becomes reduced until, eventually, the thing or situation no longer causes feelings of fear or distress. Exposure Therapy is frequently used by therapists to treat a whole slew of anxiety disorders, and variations have helped people with specific phobias or post-traumatic stress disorder.

Again, to reiterate the caveat above, neither of us are trained therapists or medical professionals, so please seek expert advice for personal treatment. Your situation may require a different approach.

In certain contexts, jumping headfirst into a 'trigger situation' could be overwhelming, cause a panic attack, and reinforce the anxiety rather than diminish it. Jonathan was fortunate in that his DIY approach seems to have worked, but with hindsight he admits he should have sought professional help when the symptoms first appeared, rather than struggle for a decade. Instead, please take heart from the knowledge that help is out there, there are things you can do, and you don't need to be crippled by anxiety forever.

Bullet train thinking

Depending on the scale of your goal, getting from a state of inertia, to hitting escape velocity in one swift move may be overwhelming or impossible. Breaking it down into chunks, and enacting incremental change, is how you'll overcome this and get to where you're going. Take a leaf out of the Japanese railways' playbook...

In the 1950s, Japan recognised that fast, long-distance, inter-city railway travel would help the country achieve the economic growth it needed after the Second World War. The challenge was set to the nation's railway engineers: build a faster train. Their first attempt managed 65 mph, but the head of the railways wanted 120 mph. This was considered impossible. Even if you put a powerful enough engine in, the train would fly off the rails as soon as the track curved.

The solution was to break this audacious stretch target down into many smaller, achievable parts: redesign the gear boxes; change the motor placement; improve aerodynamics; reduce friction; lay track with wide, banked curves; and keep testing and improving every single detail. Within ten years, they'd broken the 'impossible' 120 mph barrier. Then, they kept going. At the time of writing, the *Shinkansen* run at speeds of up to 200 mph, they are punctual to the second, quiet and comfortable, and have had no fatalities ever.

If you're struggling to see how you can get your life from a metaphorical 65 mph to 120 mph, break each problem that's slowing you down into small, resolvable parts. Tick them off, and before long you will have gotten yourself unstuck, and be on your way to achieving escape velocity and living your incredible life. You may even smash through your original targets and be on your way to 200 mph and beyond.

Goal setting

If you've ever been to any business or management training, there's a 99.9% chance you'll have heard of setting SMART goals. But in case you haven't (or if, like Jonathan, you tend to forget the good habits when in the middle of a big project) we'll provide a brief summary,

George T. Doran proposed the acronym in 1981, as a mnemonic to help when setting useful goals or tasks. The original meaning was Specific, Measurable, Assignable, Realistic, and Time-related, but this has evolved in the four decades since. There are variations, but typically the term is now understood to mean:

- **Specific**: focussed on a particular goal;
- **Measurable**: something you can track the progress of;
- **Achievable**: possible to complete;
- **Relevant**: appropriate for what you're trying to achieve;
- **Time-bound**: has some kind of timeframe or deadline.

When setting yourself goals as part of your journey from inertia to an incredible life, it can be helpful to have SMART in mind. If the task you're doing - or have set someone else - can tick off all the SMART boxes, it's more likely to get done correctly. If one or more of the factors is missing or too vague, they can slip. Lots of work may be done, but it might not be the right work. It may not be clear when the work is finished, it could be unrelated to the project's goals, or it could take far longer than expected. In any of these instances, the resulting work wouldn't just be ineffective, it would be demoralising too.

Be clear on the SMART criteria from the outset, and you improve your chances of getting to the end of a project having achieved all you wanted to achieve.

Following divorce Vicki put a financial plan in place to purchase a new home. It took two years of dedication to achieve this personal milestone, but she did it. She put a financial SMART target in place and made it happen. Yes, there were personal sacrifices, but she made it happen. If you have a goal, and you want to reach it hard enough, you can do it.[27]

Map making

We love this exercise shared with us by Karen Dennett (a Western Australia-based education, professional training, and entrepreneurial development specialist):

---

[27] Allow us to explain what we mean by 'want it enough'. It's one of those expressions that is often used in inspirational or motivational quotes, but can be unhelpful. That's because there are, quite clearly, goals we may dream of that are impossible or highly unlikely. For those, no amount of wanting it enough will suffice. We're going to ignore those 'fantasy' goals. What we're talking about is the category of 'hard, but not impossible' goals. For these, it is perfectly possible that with a lot of hard work, you may achieve them. There's a catch, though. You don't necessarily know how much effort or desire is enough. You might think you know at the start of a project, then discover it's harder than you expected. This is where the strength of your desire can make the difference between success and failure. How hard do you want it? Is that enough?

I did an exercise recently where I mapped out what I wanted in my life, what I wanted my life to look like and what sort of things I want to do. My kids are getting older now, so what leisure activities do I want to do? Where do I want to travel to? How many hours do I want to work? Then I worked out the monetary value of those things, which told me what income my business needs to achieve for me to have the life I want.

The exercise made me think about how I could maximise the time I put into my business so I can achieve that monetary target and the success I want. In turn, this made me think about my skills and how to make the most of them, with the result that I've slightly shifted how I work.

To do the exercise yourself, get your paper and pens out and 'free-write' all over the page. Put down everything that you want in your life. Just fly into it, with no editing or deleting. Because you'll add a value to each item later, it doesn't matter if you later decide something isn't really that important to you. When you've finished free writing, add a monetary value to each item. Add them up and get a total for the life you want.

Clearly, this exercise focuses on the material things. Generally, we prefer goals to be related to the intrinsic feelings we want to achieve, rather than accumulating wealth or stuff, but we also recognise that we live in a material world (as pop legend, Madonna sang), so we are going to need some money.

This exercise helps to quantify how much. Divide it by the amount you want to work and you have an hourly rate or salary to aim for.

Vision boards

Tracy Fryer (branding, graphic design, website and social media expert) is a fan of vision boards and we are too.

> I highly recommend that people have a vision board. Do it at a time when you start your business or are in goal-setting mode. It's a great focus tool. Put it somewhere you can look at it every day. I firmly believe in manifestation, so it helps if you can see your 'why' in front of you every day. For me, I've got photos of my family there.

Coaches often talk about visualisation. 'Imagine yourself crossing the finish line of the marathon,' for example. Or, 'Picture your graduation.' A vision board takes that a step further, because it pulls that aspiration out from your imagination and puts it in a physical format you can look at. Tape it to the inside of your locker, pin it up above your desk, keep it in your car. Find somewhere you will notice it everyday. It will serve as a visual reminder of what you want to achieve and help to keep you on track; especially if the going gets tough and it's harder to hold the image in your mind's eye.

Vicki agrees with Tracy. Having spent a decade doing vision boards and practising manifestation techniques, many of the goals on Vicki's vision boards have been achieved. You have to visualise what you want and treat it as if it has already happened. Pre-celebrate the achievement of those goals and think about the feeling of attainment. If you want them enough, and believe you deserve them, you can achieve your goals.

How to become an expert in something new

Achieving mastery is not just about doing your 10,000 hours. Yes, consistent effort over a period of time pays off, but there's more to it than that. In an article for the Kellogg School of Management at Northwestern University, Jessica Love outlines the five steps to becoming an expert:[28]

1. Learn from others. Find a true veteran of the game and observe what they do.
2. Find a mentor. This doesn't need to be an expert in the area you're studying, but someone who is an expert in *any* field. You're not after what they know, but how they think.

---

[28] Jessica Love, 'Take 5: How to Become an Expert in Something New', on the Kellogg Insight website. The link is in the bibliography. The article is based on the research of Jan A. Van Mieghem, Brian Uzzi, Luis Rayo, Lu Liu, Jillian Chown, Dashun Wang, Matthew D. Rocklage, Derek D. Rucker, Loran Nordgren and Steven Franconeri.

3. Do the work. Sorry, there's no shortcuts. You may have to start at the bottom, or you may already be part-way up the mountain. Either way, start climbing and keep going. The route probably won't be linear, and others can help you along the way, but you have to start moving or you won't get anywhere.

4. Explore and exploit. Don't specialise too soon. Build up a general base by experimenting and learning the fundamentals first. Then, make use of that base by going deeper into the areas you are best at.

5. Recognise the downsides. Becoming an expert can sometimes take the fun out of something you were once excited about. Have other hobbies that bring you joy.

This is all sound advice. Looking at it, you might think, 'But I don't have access to a coach.' Should it be difficult for you to find an expert you can observe in person, get creative. We live in an age in which information is everywhere. Read books and listen to podcasts (including those on topics that aren't directly related to your area of interest, because you never know where you might pick up a gold nugget of information).

Julius Yego is a javelin thrower who has won gold at the African Championships, the Commonwealth Games, and the World Championships, as well as a silver at the Olympics. He is, quite simply, one of the best javelin throwers in history. Yet Yego is from Kenya, a country not known for producing world class javelin throwers. As a child, he had no access to world class coaches, so he used YouTube. He watched videos of top athletes to learn the technique and how to train in the gym. It was as a self-taught thrower, with knowledge gained via the internet from strangers thousands of miles away, that Yego burst onto the international scene. Later, he was then able to access the best international coaches and win global medals, but that base, the foundation of his mastery, was achieved by making the most of the resources he had available to him at the time.

If Yego can become one of the best athletes in the world, using videos on the internet, what can you do?

> Reading and listening and getting other people's ideas on business is important. I started equipping myself through reading books and listening to podcasts which gave me the tools I needed to deal with those challenges.
> – Bukamu Dube, Director at Job Skills Training Academy (Perth, Western Australia)

One-pager

Stay on course by being clear about where you're going and how you want to get there. Can you distil your path to an incredible life onto one page? Like us, Usha Raman (Founder of Nexus Training Group) uses 'one-pagers':

> I believe in one-pagers, so you can see everything that's important on one page: who you are, what you do, why you do it, where you want to go, and how you're

going to get there. It's a little blueprint that is clear and simple.

The shorter and clearer, the better. Use it as the reference point you set your compass to.

Vicki has worked with many entrepreneurs who adapt the one-page approach. Some start off with a longer business plan (i.e. a business model canvas) and edit that down into a one page strategic overview. It is a great way of keeping things simple and easy to refer to.

Gonzo goals

Mention the famed 'gonzo' writer, Hunter S Thompson, and many people will picture a hedonist on drug-fuelled adventures through Las Vegas. This would not necessarily be an inaccurate image, but it only tells part of the story. Thompson was also a thinker with valuable words of wisdom to share.

In a letter to his friend Hume Logan, written when he was just 22, Thompson shared the following advice on goals, in response to a question about what one should do with one's life:

> When you were young, let us say you wanted to be a fireman. I feel reasonably safe in saying that you no longer want to be a fireman. Why? Because your perspective has changed. It is not the fireman who has changed, but you. Every man is the sum total of his

reactions to experience. As your experiences differ and multiply, you become a different man, and hence your perspective changes. This goes on and on. Every reaction is a learning process; every significant experience alters your perspective.

So it would seem foolish, would it not, to adjust our lives to the demands of a goal we see from a different angle every day? How could we ever hope to accomplish anything other than galloping neurosis?

The answer, then, must not deal with goals at all, or not with tangible goals anyway. [...] To put our faith in tangible goals would seem to be, at best, unwise. So we do not strive to be firemen, we do not strive to be bankers, nor policemen, nor doctors. WE STRIVE TO BE OURSELVES.

But don't misunderstand me. I don't mean that we can't BE firemen, bankers, or doctors - but that we must make the goal conform to the individual, rather than make the individual conform to the goal. [...] But beware of looking for goals: look for a way of life. Decide how you want to live and then see what you do to make a living WITHIN that way of life.[29]

This notion - that living according to your desires and values is the key to a happy life - is one we fully endorse. Don't think

---

[29] This is an edited extract of the full letter, written by Hunter S Thompson to Hume Logan on 22 April 1958. It can be found in *Letters of Note: An Eclectic Collection of Correspondence Deserving of a Wider Audience*, compiled by Shaun Usher, published by Canongate Books in 2013.

about a specific job or end-point. Think about a lifestyle first and live accordingly. The job, and the rest, is all just a part of that.

Where can you go for support?

If you need help, where can you find it? What are your support networks? Where are they? This will be specific to you, your business, your family, your neighbourhood and your community, so you need to work this out for yourself. You need to ensure you are clear about what you want before you ask for help. Although sometimes it is not always a linear decision making process. Also remember to be cautious about who you share your dreams with as some may not be as supportive as others. Avoid the naysayers. Advice can be from a certain perspective, based on their beliefs and experience. The advice might not necessarily be the best advice for you. Unless they are experts and have 'been there, done that', then yes, of course, take the advice.

Likewise, remember: we're all one big human family, so make sure you give back too. If someone needs your help, where can they find you?

Ask the right questions. The quality of your questions determines the quality of your answers. Instead of asking Why questions, ask How and What questions.

A lot of people might ask 'Why do we hire this

person', or 'Why did I take this step?', or 'Why did I stay in this relationship?' Instead, ask questions like 'How do I get what I want?', 'What is it I need to do next?', 'Whom do I need to speak to?', 'Where can I seek help?' I think asking the How, What, Where, Who sort of questions, instead of Why, is a really good starting place.

– Usha Raman, Founder of Nexus Training Group
(Perth, Western Australia)

Being busy versus being productive

When will you take action to work smarter, not harder? Confusing being busy with being productive is a common trap. Just because you're doing a *lot* of work doesn't mean you're doing the *right* work. Aim for quality not quantity. Different approaches work for different people. Don't get hung up on the right way of working, but do what works for you. For example, a writer doesn't need to write with their hands; they can dictate. Are there things you can do to make your work easier?

You'll know your work better than us, so we'll let you come up with your own answers to this question. As a starting point, however, we suggest that over the course of a typical work day, keep a piece of paper with you and log everything you do. The next day, review the list and circle the activity you think was the biggest waste of time (or that was useful, but could have been done more efficiently). What could you change about your routine, or how you work, to either eliminate that task, or complete it in less time? Do this, and you may reduce your stress while freeing up more time to relax or do something more productive.

The right people, the right time, the right rocket

By now, you'll have a pretty good idea of the kind of people who can help you. You may even know who they are and already have a personal or professional relationship with them. They may include your parents, romantic partners, business partners, coaches, mentors, friends, or others.

You will know what the different stages of your route to escape velocity are, what order they need to be done in, how long they'll take, and when to start each one. Work on a strategy and start pulling all your threads together. For example, this can include getting a bank account, signing up for a training course, starting to grow your network, the product design process, or your notice period for your current job! Eventually, you'll have all the knowledge you need. Don't fall into the trap of continually preparing yet never getting started. The poet, Johann Wolfgang von Goethe, said, 'Knowing is not enough, we must apply. Willing is not enough, we must do.'

Pull all your plans together, get all your systems in place, strap everything to your 'rocket' (in this case, the changes you're making to achieve the life you want) and get going. Whether it's a small step or one giant leap, start moving.

CHAPTER SEVEN

Maintaining momentum

Finish each day and be done with it. You have done what you could. Some blunders and absurdities no doubt crept in; forget them as soon as you can. Tomorrow is a new day. You shall begin it serenely and with too high a spirit to be encumbered with your old nonsense.

– Ralph Waldo Emerson, essayist and philosopher

Five factors

There are five factors that prevent people achieving their goals.

1.   Lack of focus.
2.   Lack of understanding.
3.   Lack of planning.
4.   Lack of discipline.
5.   Lack of hunger.

A lack of focus means a lack of clarity as to what it is you want. How can you accomplish your goals if you don't know what it is you want to achieve?

Once you know what you want, you need to understand what that entails. You also need to understand what it is that might stop you achieving it. This isn't just the external factors, but the internal ones. Understand your fears. Understand your previous mistakes. Understand your superpowers.

When faced with a steep slope to climb you can pull yourself straight up the mountainside, or you can step back and work out an easier route. If the steps are too far apart, add some extra steps until it becomes more manageable. This takes planning, and applies to achieving your goals, not just getting over a mountain.

Discipline doesn't mean driving yourself into the ground, day in, day out. It means sticking to the path. Keep taking steps, don't deviate from the boundaries you've set, and be true to yourself. If you stop, you won't get there. Keep moving and you will. But you have to keep moving!

Finally, you're never going to achieve a goal if you're not hungry enough. Getting the focus and understanding right can help you start off on the right path, but even if your goals are aligned with your values, it can be difficult to keep going when it gets tough. If you're losing the hunger, think back to why you started. You had the hunger once, so dig deep and retrieve it. Remember why you started on this path in the first place.

Use an academic diary

This might just be the shortest tip in the book:

- If you get stressed out by the prospect of a brand new, shiny year on every New Year's Eve, get an academic diary that runs from September to August. Then, your year won't start on 1 January.

Problem solved.

Dodge asteroids

If you're hoping to achieve escape velocity and blast into an incredible life, be prepared for asteroids: the problems and unexpected hazards that will challenge you. Author Roy T. Bennett, says:

> When you start living the life of your dreams, there will always be obstacles, doubters, mistakes and setbacks along the way. But with hard work, perseverance, and self-belief there is no limit to what you can achieve.[30]

We can hope for a smooth journey, but experience tells us that is

---

[30] Roy T. Bennett, *The Light in the Heart*, Roy Bennett, 2020.

not always likely. Get ready to identify the asteroids, pick a route through them, take evasive manoeuvres, and – potentially – take the hits.

The first strategy for dealing with asteroids is to understand what they look like and where they might be found. The exact nature of these asteroids might be unique to you, depending on your plan, but they could take the form of financial difficulties, supply-chains, customers, health issues, people that present you with problems, or other external pressures.[31] They may even be your own internal demons, belief systems, or habits. It can be easy to keep ploughing forward, head down, when you're on a mission. To dodge asteroids, you'll need to keep your head up and your eyes open. The problems won't just be those that might be actively working against you. Be alert to all possibilities and remember that the faster you get, the more of a threat stationary objects can become. Even asteroids moving in the same direction as you may prove hazardous if they're travelling slowly and you come up too fast and hit them from behind.

If you know what hazards to expect, you can put some work in to plan your route through the asteroids. You can work out how to avoid particular stressful or damaging situations, for example, or make sure that you don't need to use a particular service or supplier if you think there could be problems dealing with them. A useful task at the planning stage of any project is to carry out a pre-mortem. That is, imagine the project failing and identify all the things that have caused it to go wrong. Ask

---

[31] If your plan involves actually getting into space, then real-life asteroids, as well as metaphorical ones, will be something to worry about.

yourself, 'What's the worst that could happen?' and see if you can work out in advance how to stop that happening.

Despite all your best planning, there may still be asteroids that come out of nowhere, flying at you fast. These will require you to take evasive manoeuvres. You might not know what these asteroids look like, or when to expect them, but there are steps you can take to improve your manoeuvrability. Keep your organisation lean and flexible. Be prepared to shift production from one product to another with minimal delays. Learn how to keep your cool when someone tries to shoot you down. Adopt a mindset that is able to see the opportunities in every problem. Swerve, pivot, jump, and keep going.

BANG! A massive asteroid flies through your defences and hits you straight in the face. You lose a client, interest rates spike, you need to spend time looking after your family, or you find yourself in the middle of a Twitter pile-on and a social media sh*t-storm. Your plans are under serious threat. We hope you don't need to take too many hits, but they could happen, so you need to do what you can to improve your resiliency. We hate for this all to come down to money, but the fact is that a healthy bank balance (or a very understanding bank manager) will soften most blows. Develop Plans B, C, D, E and so on, so that you always have other options ready if Plan A has to be abandoned. Stand as strong as you can, bend if necessary, and keep striding on until you're through the asteroid belt and back in open space.

> Don't let the little things get in the way of the big picture, because they can snowball the right way or the wrong way. Brush them aside and keep moving

forward.

– Carrie Anne Forsyth, Director at Esteem Dance
Company (Perth, Western Australia)

Often, the setbacks in my business have been related to individuals. Someone will do something or try to negotiate a deal that's completely unfair. There's a few different scenarios that have happened, but it's really all about the other person. It's not personal. It's not you, it's them. They might be under a certain stress, or have pressure from their boss or something else. Remember that, and back yourself.

– Karen Dauncey, Managing Director at Blue Cherry
Online Marketing (Perth, Western Australia)

Be the CEO of your life

'Be your own boss' is good advice, but we want you to think bigger. We want you to be the CEO of your life. The Admiral, the Chair, *el Presidente*. You can still have people you are responsible to or who sit above you at work – that's OK and often hard to avoid unless you're a head of state – but when it comes to your personal wellbeing, you have to be the CEO of your life. The job description is as follows:

- Identify your purpose, or 'why'.
- Decide the strategy and make the plan.

- Choose the goals you want to tackle, and in what order.
- Sign off on the big decisions.
- Take responsibility.

It can be tough at the top, however, so make sure you look after yourself. The global wellness and health industry is huge and there is no end to the amount of stuff you can buy, all in the name of looking after yourself. But the best 'hack' is the oldest one of all and doesn't cost a penny: sleep. It is the greatest tool we have to repair and recover our minds and bodies. It's our readily accessible, built-in mechanism for growth. Babies are constantly growing, so are constantly sleeping. Assuming you're an adult, you're probably not going to get any taller from this point on, so your sleep requirements aren't going to be the same as a baby. Nonetheless, if you want personal growth, you've got to get enough rest.

Good sleep positively correlates with better innovation. Work too hard, and you can't do your best thinking. Keep your mind fresh, and the ideas will keep sparking. This is common sense, but something many of us struggle with. If you need proof to override the voice that says 'I need to keep pushing,' rest assured that the positive relationship between sleep quality and innovative behaviour has been scientifically demonstrated by Amanda Williamson, Martina Battisti, Michael Leatherbee and Jeffrey Gish in the journal of *Entrepreneurship Theory and Practice*. The 'sleep is for losers' mantra is officially dead.

The same researchers also demonstrated that mood and sleep are linked. Sleep well, and your mood will improve. Likewise, if you're in a good mood, you'll sleep better. This can be frustrating to hear if you're struggling with insomnia, but it offers a glimmer of hope: get either your mood or sleep just a little bit better, and one will feed the other. Keep the momentum moving in the right direction and you will reach the point where you're waking up supercharged and ready to do your best work.[32]

Stress and rest

Let's detour into exercise science for a moment. Physical adaptations occur when stress is followed by rest. In this context, stress refers to a movement or activity that is carried out and causes damage, whether that's tired muscles from lifting heavy weights or sore legs from running, for example. This damage is a stimulus that prompts a response from the body. This response is an adaptation made by the body to better deal with the exercise that caused the damage (the stress). Those damaged muscles, bones or joints are repaired in a way that is stronger or

---

[32] We recognise that many people suffer from insomnia. We also recognise that it can be incredibly frustrating to hear the same old advice that you will no doubt already be well aware of: don't stress about insomnia, establish a good end-of-day routine, turn off your devices and don't drink coffee, etc. This is all great advice that we would recommend, and works for most people, but some cases of insomnia are harder to shift than others. Solving cases of stubborn insomnia is beyond the scope of this book, but we're big fans of the work of Dr Nerina Ramlakhan. Jonathan attended a workshop of hers a few years ago and it made a big, positive difference to how he sleeps. Pop her name into your preferred search engine to find out more.

better suited to the activity in question. For a weightlifter, this means bigger, more powerful muscles that can better withstand the stress of lifting heavy weights. For a runner, this means stronger tendons, bones and ligaments, and muscles that are better suited to repeating an action over and over again.

Crucially, these adaptations don't happen while the stress is happening. They happen because of it, but the process of rebuilding happens after the stress, when we're resting. This is why progress cannot occur without balancing two elements: enough stress to get a response, followed by enough rest to recover and rebuild.

In practice, for athletes, this means they structure their training to balance stress and rest on the micro- through to macro-levels. For example, during a single hard training session, periods of sprinting at maximum speed will be broken up with periods of rest. Likewise, within a 24 hour period, the training session may only take up a couple of those hours, with the remainder consisting of doing very little activity. By the same reasoning, a week may involve six days with training and one day off. Then, over the course of a season or career, each big competition may be followed by a period of time off before the focus switches to the next goal. This is how the balance is struck between stress and rest in a way that prepares the athlete for peak performance. The athletes and their coaches know that it is impossible to go hard all the time. It might be possible to sustain extra work for a brief period (such as during the most important competition of the year), but not 100% effort for 100% of the time.

Hopefully you can see the parallels in your work or

personal life. To an extent, our social norms already reflect this. The majority of people in westernised countries work for a third of the day, sleep for a third of the day, and do other stuff in-between. Work on Monday to Friday is followed by two days off. We get a few weeks' worth of days off work that we can scatter throughout the year. This is how the stress of work is balanced with the need to rest and recover.

If you're working for a responsible employer in an environment with a healthy culture, maintaining this balance can be straightforward. If you're in a different kind of workplace (whether that's a small business with a boss that doesn't respect boundaries, or a massive international firm where you're expected to always be available for every client regardless of timezone) this can feel close to impossible. It can also be tough for the sole trader or entrepreneur in a service based industry who gets paid more if they work more, gets paid less if they work less, and doesn't have the benefit of paid holiday or sick days.

This balance must be maintained, though. If it tips too far into rest, then you'll get less done. Admittedly, you'll be nice and relaxed, but it might take longer to achieve your goals.

If the balance tips too far into stress, you'll be too tired to do good work, or burn out. And if you do bad work, or have a breakdown, you definitely won't get the results you want.

Think like an athlete. By all means, work hard, but don't be afraid of down time. Balance stress and rest, in a way that is sustainable and works for you (not just what other people do). Learn to listen to your body and your mind. They will tell you what they need. When your brain has been whirring, let it slow down. When your body aches, let it heal. Incorporate the stress and rest cycle into your life at all levels from the micro to the macro. Get up from your desk and have a cup of tea. Have a nap on your lunch break. Get a decent night's sleep. Enjoy the weekends. Use your annual leave and take holidays. Mix the hard with the easy. Follow dark with light, tears with laughter, and what's good for the bank balance with what's good for the soul.

It's (more than) a marathon, not a sprint

Sure, there are quick wins you can get with a short, sharp burst of energy. Powering off the start line, muscles firing, breaking the finish tape, and getting a massage with a medal around your neck, in no time at all. Relax, then look to the next goal.

Long-term, sustainable change, or the achievement of a big goal, requires less speed and more stamina: more like a marathon than a sprint. We'd go further, and say it is a marathon (or an ultramarathon) *plus* the whole training plan beforehand.

A good marathon training plan involves long runs to build endurance and speed sessions to improve your pace. But the vast majority of your runs are just about getting the miles in and making steady progress to your goal. They're the uneventful, sometimes boring runs that you go ahead and do even on the days when you'd rather be in bed or out with your mates. They're not the headline runs that people give you kudos for on social media. They're about showing up, everyday, and getting the work done.

Such a sustained effort over a long period of time requires

you to know your body. Is that achy foot a niggle that will sort itself out, or the start of an injury that will stop you from training if you carry on running? Or, are you finding it too easy because you're slacking off? Can you push the pace? Knowing when to rest and how to look after yourself is crucial if you want to get to the start line ready to perform at your best.

The same is true for your plan to achieve escape velocity. There'll be days when you make big strides forward, days when you need to take a rest, and days when you get completely lost and go in the wrong direction. In between those days, keep moving forward, even if it's just a little bit at a time. That's how you'll reach your goal. It's continual movement towards a finish line that could be far over the horizon. We might not know the route, or how long it will take to get there. We may even go backwards at points. Therefore, the ability to keep going and endure becomes crucial.

> Persistence is really, really key. You have to plan for the long run. Persistence is a muscle we can all build if we work on it.
> – Usha Raman, Founder of Nexus Training Group
> (Perth, Western Australia)

Do what works for you

Your vision of a well-rounded, balanced life, and your wellness needs, are unique to you and your situation. Don't get too hung up on the perfect way to do it. As we've already said, perfection doesn't exist. The last thing you need is to turn relaxation into something to be stressed about. There are, however, some universal basic principles that are non-negotiable:

- Eat well, most of the time.
- Move your body, frequently.
- Spend time with loved ones, often.

Beyond that, it's up to you, as demonstrated by the following examples from our Get Unstuck Fast! Viscosity Podcast guests; each of which has their own way of looking after themselves.

> I can get really caught up and super focussed on projects, and struggle to turn off. That's why I'm strategic with my calendar. It's all colour coded. Green is my time off and I schedule it before I do anything else. I put in massages every quarter, cycling trips, overnight stays, and other fun things. But I have to put them in otherwise I'll just keep working.
> – Jo Saunders, Founder of Wildfire Social Marketing
> (Perth, Western Australia)

> It took a very long time for me to really start working on myself, but I soon realised that if I was down, then nothing was happening in the business. So I needed to be my best self to make the business work. When I did, I saw results almost immediately, which was fantastic.
> The things I did were just basic health and

well-being: going to the gym, walking, moving my body. I also spend a lot of time with my loved ones. I never used to do this because I thought I didn't have the time, or I didn't make the time. Now I make a point of scheduling time off to spend with my kids, my husband and my friends.

– Bukamu Dube, Director at Job Skills Training Academy (Perth, Western Australia)

I don't do what most people do and still continue that nine to five routine: get up, go to the gym, and sit in your office or home office from nine to five. Over the last few years I've started to realise my brain works differently.

My creative genius is first thing in the morning. I'll get up normally around 5 to 5:30 and I used to go to the gym. Now I don't. That's when I will reply to my DMs, reply to messages, and write content. I'll do all that between 6 and 9 in the morning. Then I'll go to the gym at 9:15 and come back and have my breakfast.

Every day looks different, but what I've learned to do is work whenever I have the energy and not feel too bad about taking a Wednesday off to go to the beach.

– Caitriona Forde, Founder and Senior Consultant at caIT (Perth, Western Australia)

I was into fitness and sports at a young age, but not wellness. I had chocolate every day, I'll admit. But I had two operations in my twenties - one for my knee, the other for my heart - and that woke me up. What then catapulted me into my wellness journey was having really bad chronic pain. Half my face would go numb for days or I couldn't put a foot down without shooting pains. There were so many days I'd sleep on a hard floor and wish I didn't have to wake up the next morning. It was really, really bad and it was also a time when I was unhappy in my job and relationships.

So I decided to start searching for answers obsessively. Every happy person I met, I would ask 'What's your secret?' From that search I found things like life-coaching, neuro-linguistic programming [NLP], meditation, and yoga, which all opened up a whole new world for me. Life-coaching and NLP opened my eyes to all the limiting beliefs we have and the self-sabotaging decisions we make. Meditation and yoga then gave me the clarity and space to breathe. It was a beautiful journey.

I do think it is important to marry your practices with your personality, otherwise it could be really boring. I have a personality that seeks variety, so I have lots of little wellness things littered throughout my day. That's my secret, because it keeps me motivated.

Meditations and yoga, I do daily. A few times a week, I'll listen to peaceful meditation music in the background when working. I do breathing practices at night before sleeping. Having a mindful cup of tea is a nice practice. If I haven't got two minutes in a day to have one mindful cup of tea, then that is a sign that

something's wrong.
– Usha Raman, Founder of Nexus Training Group
(Perth, Western Australia)

Find a new hobby

Picture this scenario: you have a hobby you're passionate about and decide to make it your job. For the purposes of this example, let's imagine you love flower arranging at home; you get good at it and a couple of friends ask you to do the bouquets at their wedding; loads of wedding guests give you positive feedback; and you decide to become a professional florist. That's the perfect scenario, right?

Yes, it is, mostly, but there are a couple of potential negative side-effects to be aware of.

1. You come to associate the hobby you're so passionate about with the inevitable stresses of working life, or running a business.
2. If the thing you used to do to relax from work has become your work, what do you do now to relax from work?

The answer to both of these points is this: if you make your hobby your job, you need to add a new hobby to the mix. Preferably, choose something unrelated to your 'professional hobby' that requires a different frame of mind.

Jonathan loves writing and did it for personal pleasure before becoming a professional writer. To get around the pitfalls associated with making his hobby his job, he tends to keep the subjects and styles of writing separate. When writing this book, for instance, he balanced out the work-writing by writing haiku poetry or scheduling time for personal projects.

For those moments when he needs to get completely out of the writing headspace, there are a couple of options. The first is to do something physical, such as running or bouldering. The second is to do something creative that doesn't involve words, such as drawing or film photography.

The specifics aren't that important. What matters is having a pre-prepared selection of hobbies you enjoy doing that you can easily slip into when you need to forget about your work-hobby for a bit. There'll be moments when you need different activities to take your mind off work. One day, you might need to exercise. On another day, you might need to sit still or do something creative.

For the florist in our example, non-work-hobbies could involve kayaking or walking, and doing crosswords or playing the violin.

Almost all of us use a screen at work to some degree, and many will spend hours sitting down. Even a blacksmith, one of the most ancient of trades still in existence, is going to need to check their emails occasionally. Give your eyes a rest by finding a hobby that doesn't involve a screen. Stretch your body out by moving in a way you don't do at work.

It's wonderful if you can make your hobby, or something you care about, into your job. Not only do you get to do something you love all day, but you get to find new hobbies to slot into your spare time, too.

> You really can't underestimate the power of creativity as a healing tool. It's about exploring feelings, being in a mindful state, and working through something that's all yours.
> - Karen Underhill, Founder of Blue Meanies Arts and Events (Newcastle upon Tyne, UK)

Radical incrementalism

When climbers attempt to reach the summit of a large, tricky mountain, they rarely start at the bottom and head straight for the top in one go. Instead, the route is broken down into stages. The first stage might be the walk on the shallower, lower slopes. As the ground veers upwards and becomes a wall, they may clip on and start heading up. At regular points they will either loop their safety rope through a pre-laid anchor point, or attach a new one if it's a previously unclimbed route. This is an opportunity to ease off, take a breather, and assess the best way to tackle the next section. On an especially long climb, they may even rig up a tent, attach it to the side of the mountain, and settle in for the night. By breaking the big 'problem' (how to get to the top) down into a series of smaller problems, they can devise a series of smaller, sequential solutions.

This approach - breaking a big problem down into

bite-size chunks - is not unique to climbing. It's a sound, tried and tested approach that most will already be familiar with. In the business world, radical incrementalism refers to deliberately taking small steps, rather than trying to reach your ultimate goal in one big leap. This can be more sustainable, as you don't overextend yourself financially and allow time to develop your products, services, or business systems more carefully. Over time, each of these small steps adds up to significant progress. What is less well known, however, is that in addition to being an effective method of completing a project, it may also have a positive effect on our mindset.

Robert Boice is a psychology professor who studied the writing habits of other college professors, to understand which routines and approaches were most successful. What he learned is that the most productive writers wrote in smaller chunks. Rather than chain themselves to the desk for hours on end, they wrote in small chunks, between ten minutes and four hours a day. Though each individual writing session was less productive, this lighter writing routine could be sustained for longer, with a more regular rhythm, resulting in greater productivity overall.[33] Oliver Burkeman, a writer, highlighted Boice's research in his book, *Four Thousand Weeks*, equating it with the concept of radical incrementalism.[34]

Why does this approach work? Because it is less tiring, so can be continued for longer, and makes us feel good. If you break a project down into smaller tasks that can be completed at the rate of one a day, for example, you are giving yourself the

[33] Robert Boice, *How Writers Journey to Comfort and Fluency*, Praeger, 1994.
[34] Oliver Burkeman, *Four Thousand Weeks*, Farrar, Straus and Giroux, 2021.

opportunity to experience the feelings of success on a daily basis. Rather than defer the sense of accomplishment until the whole project is completed, you can get the dopamine hit of small victories every single day.

It also works because, until you reach the end of the whole project, you will always have something to start on the next day. The writer, Ernest Hemingway, is quoted as saying, 'The best way is always to stop when you are going good and when you know what will happen next. If you do that every day [...] you will never be stuck.' By adopting the radical incrementalism approach to your work and personal goals, you get to finish each day feeling good about what you've just achieved, *and* excited about tomorrow's future achievements.

Get spiky, occasionally

A well-rounded life is a comfortable life. That's a good thing. Living according to all your values, having all your needs met (with stress and rest perfectly balanced), is a lovely way to live. Such a life is something we should all aspire to.

Every now and then, however, you don't want to be well-rounded. If you want to do something new, or achieve something massive, you're going to have to get pointy or spiky.

A big project will require a big effort. If you can spread that effort out evenly, do so, but there will be times when you have to put in extra work, providing that catalyst and activation energy yourself, to get the thing done. When this is the case, unbalance yourself, pause everything else, and devote yourself to the cause.

This is easier to commit to if you know the pay off will be worth it, or the effort is only temporary. Once you've achieved the goal, soften the spikes and get round again. Avoid doing this too often, as it can tip into a burnout that you struggle to undo, but don't be afraid of doing it when necessary.

The occasional all-nighter isn't going to kill you. Repeated all-nighters might. The key is to get spiky sparingly, and to do so intentionally. Don't make it a habit. Do it because you've chosen to.

The 3am trick

During any journey from inertia to escape velocity, there will be times when you have a sticky problem to solve, or some creative thinking to do, but just can't quite get it done. No matter how much thinking you do, you can't find the answer. We've talked earlier about the importance of getting enough sleep, which is essential for recovery and growth. We've also talked about how sometimes it can be beneficial to temporarily break the good habits, in small doses, to kickstart a change.

This is where the 3am trick can help. Set an alarm for a time when you wouldn't normally be awake. Get out of bed, sit down (or walk around) and write down (or dictate) whatever comes to mind when you think about the problem. Don't look at or critique what you've written, but get down everything you can, put it away, then go back to bed and attempt to sleep.

Yes, there's a chance your brain might still be fizzing too much to sleep straight away. However, if you're resorting to the 3am trick, it's likely the problem was disrupting your sleep anyway. If that's the case, this is just one more restless night to attempt to get the job done.

When you get up properly, at your standard time, to face the day, you can look over what you wrote. You might not have created instant gold, but hopefully, there'll at least be the seed of a solution scribbled down. If so, nurture that seed and see what ideas grow.

If not, there'll at least be a whole load of bad ideas that you'll know won't work. Head in the opposite direction to those and you might come across an answer.

There isn't some particular magic about 3am that means this exercise has to be done at this time. There's no reason why you couldn't do it at a different time. The principle is to jolt your brain out of your existing thought ruts by doing some thinking at a different time or in a different place. If you do it in the middle of the night, when you've been asleep and your brain hasn't yet been taken over by thoughts of all the other stuff in your life, you may find a clarity that you wouldn't otherwise have (even if you're feeling a bit sleepy and foggy-headed).

It's hard when things are tough as you can get stuck in a moment and be so focussed on where you are. You have to press pause, step aside, and get yourself outdoors, work out or do something else. Get back to what you used to love.

For me, I've rediscovered cycling and love being outdoors. When I'm doing it I'm completely disconnected, in the fresh air, and seeing stuff around me. I do it with my husband as 'date time'. It's about stepping out of your 'stuckness' and doing something else unrelated to your business. Getting outdoors changes your perspective, changes your energy, and can help you find the solutions you need.

– Jo Saunders, Founder of Wildfire Social Marketing
(Perth, Western Australia)

Go for a walk

If the 3am trick doesn't work for you, or you'd rather not set your alarm for such an antisocial hour, there are gentler options for getting unstuck. Meditation is wonderful. It's tried and tested over thousands of years, and we would encourage everyone to do it. However, we recognise that the classic notion of guided meditation or sitting in silence is not for everyone, or may not always be the right approach. Rather than sit down, change your surroundings and head out for a walk (like Jo Saunders, as mentioned above). When it comes to dealing with anxiety, research has shown no significant difference between meditation when sat down, or meditation when walking.[35]

---

[35] Meghan K Edwards, Simon Rosenbaum & Paul D Loprinzi, 'Differential Experimental Effects of a Short Bout of Walking, Meditation, or Combination of Meditation on State Anxiety Among Young Adults',

Maintaining momentum - **199**

Ideally, you'd do so in a calm, natural environment, but this isn't essential. As long as you're being mindful and calm, it doesn't matter much whether you're sitting in a room with incense burning, gently strolling through a park, or doing a meditative craft such as drawing or weaving.

Take the power back

Let's acknowledge something important: sometimes, bad things happen to people for reasons that are not their fault. We don't deny that. None of us get to be the arbiters who decide what someone else should feel about events that have happened to them. We will never deny anyone the right to feel they have been made a victim, and we will never blame any victim for what has taken place. This is important to acknowledge, as so many self-help guides tell readers that they can simply choose not to be a victim. This point of view is unhelpful, disrespectful and potentially dangerous. Trauma is not a matter of mindset. Abusers rarely ask for permission. Scars are not optional.

We might not always get a choice about what happens to us, but we can do work to shape how we think about it and we do get to decide how we act. The transition from a state of being stuck to living an incredible life requires you to be in charge of the process. During this journey you may have little control over other people or events. Therefore, you absolutely must take the

---

American Journal of Health Promotion, Vol. 32, Issue 4, 2017.

power back over your body and mind.

Beyond some basic genetic coding to keep us alive – breathing, eating, reacting to pain, etc. – we are born with an almost-blank slate of behaviours. Nearly everything we do or think is learned. We either learn it ourselves or we're taught it by others. Even with the best intentions, our loved ones can pass on their own fears or negative modes of thinking. Fortunately, we can learn new behaviours or unlearn those we want to discard.

Likewise, the stories we tell ourselves (or the stories we've been told about ourselves) can be rewritten. As children, we are sponges and absorb everything around us. It is desperately unfair that sometimes people (adults, or other children) say false, cruel or unhelpful things to children that they might carry for the rest of their lives. It's so sad that confident children are told to shut up; that children who struggle in a conventional education system are told they're stupid; that children from poorer backgrounds are told to set lower aspirations; or that any child carries shame for anything they have no responsibility for.

These examples - and plenty of others we can all recognise - may resonate with you personally. Take the story you've been told about yourself, write it down, then cross it out. Get a new sheet of paper and write your own story. Every time you find yourself slipping back into the old modes of thinking or behaving - and you will, because it takes time to reprogramme the habits of a lifetime - repeat the exercise. Cross out the old lies and rewrite your new truth.

The lessons and the stories you're rejecting and rewriting are the macro life factors you can take control of. On a micro, everyday level, remember your emotions are yours and yours alone. Resist the attempts of others to dictate how you feel.

When Vicki was reaching a 'significant' birthday, she reflected on her life and thought about her dreams as a child of becoming a DJ, an entrepreneur and teacher. Her love for music had been pushed aside for other pursuits, because she believed the story that she couldn't combine it with a 'professional' career. To rewrite that story, Vicki decided to purchase DJ equipment, and two weeks later got her first gig for 150 people. She then went on to set up a lifestyle business performing in Perth, Western Australia: a side hustle that became a sustainable income stream.

> It doesn't matter if you're Elon Musk, Jeff Bezos, or someone kicking about on the street: no one gets to dictate how you feel. Only you determine your own emotions. You can be the wealthiest person on earth or you could be the poorest person on earth. You get to decide how you feel and who to surround yourself with. Nothing you ever do can be seen from space. We're all insignificant in the grand scheme of things, so don't worry about things that will be forgotten. Get back to the fundamentals and simplicity. Choose what you want to do. Choose how you want to feel. And don't dwell on negative thoughts.
> – Bryn Walbrook, Freelance Brand Strategist (London, UK)

When my husband died of a brain haemorrhage, I just reacted. I'm a strong person, I think on my feet, I'm a natural leader, and I thought about how I could turn this tragedy into a positive thing. Previously, I'd have never imagined I would be running bereavement workshops or bereavement projects.

- Karen Underhill, Founder of Blue Meanies Arts and
Events (Newcastle upon Tyne, UK)

Confront your tendencies

Following your gut instincts is, usually, a good thing to do. Deep down, we tend to know what is right for us. Except, of course, when our gut is being unhelpful and trying to get us to fall into bad habits. If your progress is stalling, it's possible you may be subconsciously self-sabotaging. Don't be hard on yourself if this is the case. As we've said, it takes time to change the way our minds work.

A useful strategy for getting unstuck is to identify your tendencies and inclinations and force yourself to do the opposite. For example, if you have a tendency to flit or a desire to change - frequently changing jobs, moving house, or ending relationships - it can be worthwhile seeing what happens, or how you feel, when you do the opposite. Don't move, stay still.

Likewise, if you're reluctant to change, or tend to say 'no' to new opportunities, see what happens when you try something different. There will probably be a period when you feel uncomfortable, and have to fight the urge to stop the experiment. This is your cue that you need to give it just that little bit longer, as you're on the verge of a breakthrough. Get to the point when your instincts have quietened down and you can view the situation with a rational mind, free of emotional impulses. One of two things will happen, and they're both positive:

1.   You won't enjoy it, it won't work, and you'll reaffirm that your instincts are to be trusted.
2.   You'll discover a new way of being, a new skill, or a new insight you can use, that leads to good things.

Either way, it's a win-win situation.

Gratitude

Everyone, but especially people who tend to the negative, should cultivate a 'gratitude mindset'. This doesn't always come easily, so you may have to train yourself until it becomes an automatic habit. To do it, literally count your blessings.

Keep a small notebook and pencil by your bed.[36] Before you go to sleep, take a few minutes to record the good things that happened in your day. If nothing obvious and specific comes to mind, opt for something general. 'I'm grateful for my health', for example.

It can be deep ('I'm grateful for my loving relationship')

---

[36] Unlike a phone, a notebook isn't going to disrupt your sleep. And unlike a pen, a pencil won't leak ink on your sheets.

204 - The Momentum Mindset

or relatively shallow ('I'm grateful that Bill didn't eat the last banana'). It doesn't matter too much. What's important is that you start with 'I'm grateful…' so that you can frame whatever comes next in purely positive terms.

There will be days when nothing good happens! On those days, look for something, anything, that you can be grateful for, even if it's 'I'm grateful that the car crash wasn't worse!' There's always a silver lining.

The results can include increased dopamine and reduced stress levels. In turn, this can lead to lower blood pressure and inflammation.[37] So it's not just a nice thing to do, it can be beneficial to your health, too.

At the end of each week, circle your 'gratitude of the week' and reflect upon it to give yourself an extra boost of positivity (which can be extra helpful on a Sunday night before getting back to work on Monday). When you've filled your notebook, flick through it and enjoy the tangible reminder of all the things you have to be grateful for.

> I have gotten into the habit of keeping a journal. A big part of it is about self reflection. I find it really useful, even if it's just five minutes a day before work. Wake up a little bit early, do a bit of exercise, then sit down and spend time with yourself as the sun comes up. Write down what it is you're grateful for. It can be something really simple, such as: I'm still able to breathe; I have a notebook in front of me and I can afford a pen; The sun is shining. Then answer 'How

---

[37] There are details of studies and articles on this in the bibliography.

do I want to be today?' and set your intentions.
– Dr Christopher Kueh, Design Abilities Specialist
(Perth, Western Australia)

Super-gratitude

For an extra-powerful gratitude super-boost, share the love. If you've written something nice about someone in your gratitude journal, tell them!

You can do this however you want, but we reckon a hand-written, posted thank you letter is about as good as it gets. Not only will you get the emotional boost from thinking about what you're grateful for, but the recipient will receive an unexpected surprise to give them a lift too. How about sending one a month?

Jonathan had the pleasure of running a training course for a group of young theatre makers on how they can raise money for their artistic projects. At the end of the session, as he was preparing to pack up and say his goodbyes, his colleague, Clarice Montero, the facilitator, asked each workshop participant in turn to say what they were grateful to Jonathan for. This is something the group had done for each of the workshop facilitators who had spoken to the group during this project.

To have a dozen people say nice things about you is an unusual experience, but perhaps it shouldn't be. Once he got over the initial discomfort of unexpectedly being placed at the centre of a group gratitude-giving experience, Jonathan appreciated the act and, understandably, left the workshop feeling really good about himself and the work he had done.

Why isn't this more commonplace? Admittedly, there are some contexts in which it would be neither appropriate nor practical. One hundred attendees of a lecture giving thanks to the lecturer could double the amount of time required on the room booking. However, for a small group workshop, such as the one Jonathan ran, or other scenarios in which someone benefits from another's work, effort or advice, intentional gratitude stating could be a powerful way to finish proceedings. A 'thank you' is (or should be) a standard, polite statement, but the details of what someone is being thanked for are either implied or not given. They are rarely specified in such an overt manner. 'Thank you. I am grateful to you for X, Y or Z.'

We'd encourage you to try it out and make a habit of it. At the very least, whoever you are thanking will walk away from your interaction feeling good about themselves. At best, it'll catch on and you'll create a culture within your business or community of gratitude sharing that will uplift everyone.

Plan, do, review

It's a useful habit to build review periods into your schedule. The timing of these will depend on the nature of your work, but they're essential if you want to do not just your best work, but the *right* work. A task can be broken down into the following stages:

- **Problem**: there is a thing that needs to be addressed or a goal to be achieved.
- **Awareness**: we become aware of the problem.
- **Solution**: we identify what we would like this situation to look like.
- **Plan**: we work out how to achieve the solution.
- **Do**: we carry out the plan.
- **Review**: we check that we've achieved the solution, ask whether it could have been done better, and look around to see if there are any other problems to be aware of.

If we're caught up in the daily grind, the review stage can get lost. It's easier in the short term to think, 'Bang. Done. On to the next thing.' But without the review stage we won't know for certain whether we've done it as well as we could. We also won't know if the next thing on our to-do list is actually the best thing we could do next.

This is especially important if each task is a step on your way to achieving a bigger goal, such as achieving escape velocity. You could be firing away, getting loads done, but if you don't review it, that work could be ineffective or take you in the wrong direction.

Pause, look around, make adjustments to your course as necessary, then go again.

Stay true to yourself

Stop focusing on others. You don't have to be the next Richard Branson, Ruth Bader Ginsburg, Maya Angelou or Usain Bolt. Be yourself, not a cardboard cutout of someone else. Do not compare yourself to others. Celebrate your uniqueness. Have the confidence to back yourself. Focus on your own goals and get stuff done.

You are what you do

Paraphrasing the writer Oscar Wilde, the actor Stephen Fry said, 'We are not nouns, we are verbs.' That is, we are not *things*, but people who *do* things.

This works in two directions. If your goal is to act/write/teach (delete as applicable), it's not enough to call yourself an actor/writer/teacher. You have to act/write/teach. On top of that, if you want to get really good at it, you're going to need to do a lot of it.

Flip it around, and it also shows we don't need to be imprisoned by our nouns. If you don't want to be one thing, you just have to do something else.

Think of yourself as a verb and be liberated. You can do what you want to do; you just have to do it.

Return to self-reflection

The self-reflective questions throughout this book have been designed with the expectation you will return to them. How you do so is up to you, but we suggest scheduling a regular review in your diary. Perhaps every few months, every year, or at the conclusion of a significant project, return to the questions and ask yourself if your answers still hold true.

People change. You, and the people you interact with, will change over time. This means your answers to the questions you've been asking of yourself may also change. This is not a problem. It's quite the opposite. It indicates growth and evolution as your perspective changes with experience. On the same note, don't be disheartened if your answers don't change. That just indicates a certainty around your purpose and aims that indicates you are still doing the right thing for you.

There's no right or wrong here, because this is about you. They're *your* answers, for you to do what you want with! Regularly reviewing them serves two purposes:

1.   It is an opportunity to remind yourself of your 'why' and re-motivate yourself. This is a brief break point to pause what you're doing, look around, and take a breath – something we don't always do when in the middle of a busy phase of work or life pressures.

2.   It is an opportunity to make adjustments to your direction of travel. Is this still what you want? Are you doing it in the most effective way? To carry on blindly, following the course you set on Day 1, with no

allowances for changing circumstances or wishes, is not the best way to achieve escape velocity. Accepting that adjustments need to be made can be difficult for some people. Perfectionists with a particularly determined streak may fall in the trap of considering any kind of adjustment as a compromise or failure. This is false thinking. You might yet achieve great things, but by stubbornly sticking to the original plan, they may not end up being the things that are right for you at the point you achieve them. Don't be a slave to your own plan. To echo the point above, it's *your* plan for you to do what you want with.

Keep your original answers to hand. When you get to your review day, block out some time, minimise distractions, sit down, and look at your progression with self-compassion. If you've gone off-track, that's OK. Realign yourself and get going again. If you're flying, smashing all the targets you've set yourself, bravo! But make sure you slow down for long enough to congratulate yourself, for the big wins and the small ones.

Waypoints

A long path can take years to walk. During that time it is easy to lose energy, lose hope, lose motivation, or lose your way. Avoid these pitfalls by breaking the route into sections and pausing to read your map and check your compass. Here are our suggested waypoints:

- Set key performance indicators (KPIs) that you check every year. If it doesn't get measured, it doesn't get done.
- Every 90 days, set interim targets to achieve your annual goals.
- Break those blocks down into daily tasks to achieve, remembering to keep them SMART.

Write this down in your diary and stick to the dates. The meetings you have with yourself are the most important meetings you'll have, so prioritise them. Book them in now. (If you're someone who gets a little freaked out by New Year's resolutions (and we know a few), you don't have to do your annual review at the changing of each calendar year. You can pick any day you want.) Further to the above, these pointers will keep you on track:

- Do more of the actions that will help you achieve your KPIs (and do fewer of the actions that won't).
- Seek help if you need it – from a doctor, coach, therapist, romantic partner, child, colleague, boss, client, or guru. Fit the expert to your needs.
- Your time is valuable, so protect it.
- Be ruthless with clutter: both physical and mental. Recycle it, file it, or archive it.
- Outsource what you can. For example, if you don't have time for, or don't enjoy admin, find someone else to do

it. There are people who thrive on administrative tasks,[38] so use them if you can. Consider this: if it costs you £100 to pay someone to do something you don't want to do, but you're able to earn an extra £200 in the time you free up, then it's money well spent.

- Work smarter, not harder, and enjoy all the things you love in your life. Celebrate the milestones and waypoints you pass on your journey, and the wins you achieve. Acknowledge the things you have to be grateful for.

Bryn Walbrooks's approach works well for him:

> Every six months, and at the end of every year, I grade myself on the goals I've set. The areas are personal life, professional life, financial and adventure. I can use this to see how I've grown in each of those areas, then set three things in each of those areas that I'd like to do.
>
> For example, I did quite a lot of Muay Thai and wanted to compete at a semi-professional level. That was one of my goals. I wanted to take up CrossFit this year, so I took up CrossFit and I'm really enjoying it. I wanted to go to three countries I've never been to. The exercise is important because it's so hard to step away from and see the bigger picture. Slow incremental gains are really hard to visualise because we only live in the present and this helps.
>
> – Bryn Walbrook, Freelance Brand Strategist
> (London, UK)

---

[38] All such administrative wizards are absolute legends in our opinion!

CHAPTER EIGHT

Pre-launch checks

Twenty years from now, you will be more disappointed by the things that you didn't do than by the ones you did do. So throw off the bowlines. Sail away from the safe harbour. Catch the trade winds in your sails. Explore. Dream. Discover.

– Mark Twain, writer and entrepreneur

Your incredible life-story

By adopting the strategies outlined above, we've made significant steps on the way to achieving our own incredible lives.

Jonathan has mostly overcome the mental health issues that caused him so many problems (there's still some work to do there, but the bulk of the hard work has been done). He has a happy, healthy relationship with Heather, his wife. He is doing work he feels proud of. And he feels grateful to the people who have helped him along the way.

Vicki is now with a loving partner where 'reciprocity' is their collective mantra. They have a base in Chelsea, London and a dog called Leo. Vicki now works and lives between the UK and Australia: the best of both worlds. Her client base is growing and she continues to help individuals and companies overcome their state of stationary inertia and build a momentum mindset. Her children are still and always will be her biggest 'why'.

We're not sharing these personal stories to brag, or show off. We know that we're not inherently more or less special than anyone else out there. As we've described throughout this book, we've faced the same or similar issues to countless other people out there. We're not perfect. We'll always be flawed human beings with our own sh*t to deal with and things we would still like to change about ourselves and the world around us. We've overcome personal challenges and will inevitably have more that we have to deal with in the future.

But we're both living according to our own values, working towards the goals we have set ourselves. We're carrying the escape velocity momentum and are prepared to dodge any asteroids that come our way. And that feels incredible.

Now you know our journeys, and where we've got to, what about you? Ask yourself, 'what incredible life-story are you going to write for yourself?'

Take action to fulfil your purpose

We have written a lot about thinking and reflecting so far. This is an essential part of the process, but it needs to be followed with action. To live an incredible life, you need to align that action with your values. You'll be happier if you remain true to yourself by matching the things you do with the things you care about. This may seem impossible, especially if you're stuck in a tough situation and having to compromise on your values. We understand that. Sometimes the most important personal changes are the hardest ones to make. So start small and build speed gradually.

To help you, here's a checklist that summarises the key tasks or action points we've mentioned:

- ☐ Imagine an incredible life.
- ☐ Write down what you want to change.
- ☐ Write down your fears.
- ☐ Identify the superpowers that led to your successes.
- ☐ Do the 'So What?' exercise.
- ☐ Do the *ikigai* exercise.
- ☐ Examine your previous choices.
- ☐ Think about the qualities you admire in others.
- ☐ Do an EMP assessment (visit www.govlm.com/emp)
- ☐ Schedule time to reflect.
- ☐ Do a life audit.
- ☐ Exorcise your past demons.
- ☐ Do something that scares you.
- ☐ Do something creative.

☐ Design your team.
☐ Get help from a health professional, if required.
☐ Prepare your No script.
☐ Detox, declutter and streamline your life.
☐ Make adaptable, SMART plans that work for you.
☐ Schedule reviews.
☐ Try a new hobby.
☐ Go for a walk.
☐ Start a gratitude journal.
☐ Say 'thank you' to someone.

It has been our intention when writing this book to create a resource that will help you to:

- Define your values.
- Identify what you can do to live according to those values.
- Devise a plan to achieve that value-driven life.
- Develop the tools to maintain momentum should the journey prove difficult.

This is all to help you get unstuck, achieve escape velocity, and live the incredible life that you deserve.

Now, it's up to you. There may never be a perfect time to change your life, so now is as good a time as any to take the first step.

Go on.

Start walking.

Epilogue: Anticipation, activation, achievement

The ground shakes, the air fills with smoke and noise, and a trail is drawn across the sky. Onlookers follow its progress from afar, gaze rising from horizon to zenith. Anticipation, activation, achievement.

A space shuttle on the back of a launch rocket weighs more than 2,000,000 kg. That's a number that's far too big to be meaningful to most of us, but it's big. At the time of writing this, in 2023, it's been twelve years since the last such launch, but it still remains the heaviest thing to be put into space on the back of a rocket. Even moving the shuttle and rocket assembly from the hangar to the launch pad takes a phenomenal amount of energy and effort, crawling on a specially-built transporter at a speed of just 1.6 km/h. Yet, with the application of an almighty burst of energy, provided by the combustion of ammonium perchlorate and atomised aluminium powder, directed down into the ground, it can lift off and ascend skywards, leaving the ground behind. Accelerating further, up to 29,000 km/h, it can reach a height where it can orbit the planet with no further effort.

Up high above the Earth and far from where it started, there is no air to provide resistance and the effects of gravity are minimal. Now, after the initial controlled explosion that got it off the ground, the rocket can continue forwards, with far less energy expenditure, carried by its own momentum and only requiring occasional adjustments and corrections to its course. In the same moment, elsewhere on Earth, in many different situations, inertia is overcome, momentum is built, and velocity is achieved.

A cheetah watches a herd of antelope. One of them is limping. Eyes on the target, the cheetah waits, waits, waits... GO! Neural impulses fire muscle fibres. From stationary to full stride in the blink of an eye. The antelope scatters, but the cheetah is faster. Within seconds it has made up the distance, struck out with sharp claws and terrible jaws, made the kill, and is back at rest. Anticipation, activation, achievement.

A cartoon elephant with a successful career as an aviator decides to dream bigger. This world is too small for him and he wants to go further than any elephant has been before. He sits down with his mouse mentor and his crow coaching team, and they start planning.

A rabbit decides that the hutch he was given isn't for him and rebels against his confined existence. He moves out and starts building a new home, under the garage, so he can live life on his own terms.

In the UK, Jonathan decides he is fed up with feeling scared, anxious, and nervous. He knows that the change has to come from within, but the prospect of doing so is terrifying. On this day, however, he decides to conquer his fears by embracing them, and to rewrite his attitude to life. He makes an appointment with a dentist and in doing so takes a small first step towards overcoming anxiety and claustrophobia.

In Australia, Vicki wakes, shaken by a dream, a nightmare she fears is prophetic. She has known for sometime now that something – her environment, her attitude, her actions? – needs to change. But it is scary. Even though her current situation is a negative one, and she is not living how she wants to live, there is a perverse comfort in maintaining the status quo. It's the devil you know. Change is hard, even if it is a change we desire. This morning is different. Enough is enough.

Plans are drawn up, the target is identified, an inward breath to prime the body and mind. This is the anticipation stage.

The rocket fuel ignites, neural impulses fire, comfort zones are breached. Flying, striding, gliding. It is difficult. Of course it is. This is the activation stage when the greatest input of energy is required to change the state of being. From zero right up to escape velocity.

And then? Sustained momentum. Forward progress. Onwards. Higher. Greater. It's not all friction-free, smooth and flawless as nothing ever is, but the necessary course corrections are easier than the initial impulse to begin.

Into space, the target reached, a goal attained. This is the achievement stage. Your life has changed for the better.

Congratulations! Welcome to your incredible life.

Thank you

To Jonathan, what a pleasure it has been to work with you; we did it! To my clients and podcast contributors; you are incredibly inspiring people. Thank you to Tracy Fryer and the team at Design Studio Perth for designing the cover, and Karen Underhill for your creative input on the initial ideas. To my children, William and Oliver. I love you. Be kind and don't ever give up on your dreams. To my mother who enabled me to question the status quo and ignited my curiosity and my will to inspire and develop people. To the love of my life, Will King. Without you this book would have remained unwritten.

Finally to you, the reader: give yourself permission to achieve escape velocity.

– Vicki

Thanks are due to so many people, but especially Heather and my family. Thanks to Vicki for asking me to join her on this journey. Thanks to Will for his support of this project. Thanks to Richard Askwith for his advice. Thanks to the proofreaders (Nicola Moses, Tony King, Linda Hand & Danielle Meikle). And thanks to you, for reading.

– Jonathan

Bibliography

Books

Alan Badiou, *Happiness*, Bloomsbury, 2019.

Roy T. Bennett, *The Light in the Heart*, Roy Bennett, 2020.

Robert Boice, *How Writers Journey to Comfort and Fluency*, Praeger, 1994.

Oliver Burkeman, *Four Thousand Weeks*, Farrar, Straus and Giroux, 2021.

Charles Duhigg, *Smarter Faster Better*, Penguin Random House, 2016.

Carol Dwek, *Mindset: How to Fulfil Your Potential*, Robinson, 2012.

Victor E. Frankl, *Man's Search for Ultimate Meaning*, Plenum, 1997.

Steven C. Hayes & Spencer Smith, *Get Out of Your Mind and Into Your Life*, New Harbinger Publications, 2005.

Soren Kierkegaard, *The Concept of Anxiety*, WW Norton & Co, 2015 (first published 1844).

Haruki Murakami, *Novelist as a Vocation*, Harvill Secker, 2022 (published in Japanese by Switch Publishing Co., Ltd. in 2015).

Kristin Neff, *Self-Compassion*, Hodder & Stoughton, 2011.

DBC Pierre, *Release the Bats*, Faber & Faber, 2016.

Robert M. Pirsig, *Zen and the Art of Motorcycle Maintenance*, Harper Collins, 1974.

Nerina Ramlakhan, *Tired but Wired*, Souvenir Press, 2010.

Nassim Nicholas Taleb, *Antifragile*, Penguin, 2012.

Shaun Usher, ed., *Letters of Note*, Canongate Books, 2013

Articles

Emma Bradshaw, James Conigrave, Ben Steward, Kelly Ferber, Philip Parker & Richard Ryan, 'A Meta-Analysis of the Dark Side of the American Dream: Evidence for the Universal Wellness Costs of Prioritising Extrinsic over Intrinsic Goals', *Journal of Personality and Social Psychology*, 2022.

Edward Deci & Richard Ryan, 'Self-determination theory: A macrotheory of human motivation, development, and health', *Canadian Psychology / Psychologie canadienne*, Vol. 49, Issue. 3, 2008.

Adam Doerrfeld, Natalie Sebanz & Maggie Shiffrar, 'Expecting to lift a box together makes the load look lighter', *Psychological Research*, Vol. 76, Issue 4, 2012.

Christina M. DuBois, Scott R. Beach, Todd B, Kashdan, Maren B. Nyer, Ekyse R. Park, Christopher M. Celano & Jeff C. Huffman, 'Positive psychological attributes and cardiac outcomes: associations, mechanisms, and interventions', *Psychosomatics*, Vol. 53, Issue 4, 2012.

Christina M. DuBois, Oriana Vesga Lopez, Eleanor E. Beale, Brian C. Healy, Julia K. Boehm & Jeff C. Huffman, 'Relationships between positive psychological constructs and health outcomes in patients with cardiovascular disease: A systematic review', *International Journal of Cardiology*, Vol. 195, 2015.

Meghan K. Edwards, Simon Rosenbaum & Paul D. Loprinzi, 'Differential Experimental Effects of a Shout Bout of Walking, Meditation, or Combination of Walking and Meditation on State Anxiety Among Young Adults',

American Journal of Health Promotion, Vol. 32, Issue 4, 2018.

Szu-Chi Huang & Jennifer Aaker, 'It's the journey, not the destination: How metaphor drives growth after goal attainment', *Journal of Personality and Social Psychology*, Vol. 117, Issue 4, 2019.

Eric S. Kim, Kaitlin A. Hagan, Francine Grodstein, Dawn L. DeMeo, Immaculata De Vivo & Laura D. Kubzansky, 'Optimism and Cause-Specific Mortality: A Prospective Cohort Study', *American Journal of Epidemiology*, Vol. 185, Issue 1, 2017.

Eric S. Kim, Jennifer K. Sun, Nansook Park, Laura D. Kubzansky & Christopher Peterson, 'Purpose in life and reduced risk of myocardial infarction among older U.S. adults with coronary heart disease: a two-year follow-up', *Journal of Behavioral Medicine*, Vol. 36, 2013.

Laura D. Kubzansky, Jeff C. Huffman, Julia K. Boehm, Rosalba Hernandez, Eric S. Kim, Hayami K. Koga, Emily H. Feig, Donald M. Lloyd-Jones, Martin E. P. Seligman & Darwin R. Labarthe, 'Positive Psychological Well-Being and Cardiovascular Disease: JACC Health Promotion Series', *Journal of the American College of Cardiology*, Vol. 72, Issue 12, 2018.

Marily Oppezzo & Daniel L. Schwartz, 'Give your ideas some legs: The positive effect of walking on creative thinking', *Journal of Experimental Psychology: Learning, Memory, and Cognition*, Vol. 40, Issue 4, 2014.

Robert Rogers & Stephen Monsell, 'The costs of a predictable switch between simple cognitive tasks', *Journal of*

Experimental Psychology: General, Vol. 124, 1995.

Simone Schnall, Kent D. Harber, Jeanine K. Stefanucci & Dennis R. Proffitt, 'Social Support and the Perception of Geographical Slant', *Journal of Experimental Social Psychology*, Vol. 44, Issue 5, 2008.

Karina Schumann & Michael Ross, 'Why women apologize more than men: gender differences in thresholds for perceiving offensive behavior', *Psychological Science*, Vol. 21, Issue 11, 2010.

Nancy L. Sin, 'The Protective Role of Positive Well-Being in Cardiovascular Disease: Review of Current Evidence, Mechanisms, and Clinical Implications', *Current Cardiology Reports*, Vol. 18, 2016.

Amanda Williamson, Martina Battisti, Michael Leatherbee & Jeffrey Gish, 'Rest, Zest, and My Innovative Best: Sleep and Mood as Drivers of Entrepreneurs' Innovative Behavior', *Entrepreneurship Theory and Practice*, Vol. 43, Issue 3, 2019.

Kaitlin Woolley & Ayelet Fishbach, 'Motivating Personal Growth by Seeking Discomfort', *Psychological Science*, Vol. 33, Issue 4, 2022.

Online

Teresa M. Amabile & Steven J. Kramer, 'The Power of Small Wins', *Harvard Business Review*, May 2011, https://hbr.org/2011/05/the-power-of-small-wins

Jessica Love, 'Take 5: How to Become an Expert in Something New', *Kellogg Insight*, 25 October 2021, https://insight.kellogg.northwestern.edu/article/take-5-be

come-an-expert

Steve Magness, 'Why We Need to Seek Out Discomfort', *The Growth Equation*, https://thegrowtheq.com/why-we-need-to-seek-out-disco mfort/

Amy Morin, 'Women Really Do Apologize More Than Men. Here's Why (and It Has Nothing to Do With Men Refusing to Admit Wrongdoing)', *Inc.*, 26 March 2019, https://www.inc.com/amy-morin/women-really-do-apolo gize-more-than-men-heres-surprising-reason-why-and-it-h as-nothing-to-do-with-self-esteem.html

Jo Nash, 'How to Set Healthy Boundaries & Build Positive Relationships', *PositivePsychology.com*, 5 January 2018, https://positivepsychology.com/great-self-care-setting-hea lthy-boundaries

Candace Plattor, 'Authenticity vs. Attachment: Which One Will You Choose?', *Recovery.org*, 9 September 2019, https://recovery.org/pro/articles/authenticity-vs-attachme nt-which-one-will-you-choose/

'Giving thanks can make you happier', *Harvard Health Publishing*, 14 August 2021, https://www.health.harvard.edu/healthbeat/giving-thank s-can-make-you-happier

'Multitasking: Switching costs', *American Psychological Association*, 20 March 2006, https://www.apa.org/topics/research/multitasking

'12 New Year's resolutions', *Monocle*, Issue 159, 2022, https://monocle.com/magazine/issues/159/12-new-year-s -resolutions/

Online support

Find sources of support on the Free Resources page of our website: https://www.govlm.com/freeresources

Alternatively visit https://www.govlm.com to find out more about the VLM Momentum Mindset Coaching Programs and Online Events.

Space for your notes